To Rita
a great event
in my life's
journey — See page 126

Ray

Short Shorts 'n' Stanzas

A Compilation of Short Stories,
Essays and Poems.

Ray Toney

Short Shorts 'n' Stanzas

© 2013 Ray Toney

ISBN: 978-1-61170-132-6

Printed in the USA and UK on acid-free paper.

 **Robertson Publishing**™
www.RobertsonPublishing.com

To purchase additional copies of this book go to:
   amazon.com
   barnesandnoble.com
   www.rp–author.com/toney

DEDICATION

This for Brian and Erin who only know their father from the time of their being. If they ever wonder what he was like as a kid, what kind of scrapes he got into and what life was like in the thirties and forties when he grew up, this is a small sampling.

Also included are essays and stories on happenings in later times. Some of it with real meaning to me and some, just plain whimsical in nature.

Ray Toney,
Los Gatos, California

ACKNOWLEDGEMENTS

Grateful thanks to all those who gave their time and talents to creating the sum of this book.

Dori Stephenson for her keen proofreading eye, Brian Scott Toney for suggestions and assistance with the cover art and Alicia Robertson for her guidance and direction.

Cast
In Order of Appearance

Baby Raymond and "Bonnie"

RAYMOND'S RABBIT

He was a quiet baby. Except when the aunts and uncles helped to hold him down flat on the kitchen table, while his mother tried to administer the Argyrol nose drops the doctor had prescribed for his nasal congestion.

He would cry and scream, kick and twist his head back and forth to prevent the nasty tasting medicine from getting into his nose. The family members were only trying to help him get over the cold he had caught from his cousin Kenny.

It was a feeling of helplessness he would never quite get over; being held down.

He enjoyed exploring his grandfather and grandmother's spacious house and gardens. Even as a toddler, he would crawl, or walk, unsteadily, out among the many rabbit hutches that filled most of the rear yard.

Grandpa Joe was a lineman for the telephone company, back in those days, but raised New Zealand White rabbits to supplement his income.

With a large household, comprised of his wife, two of her grown daughters, Rose and Thelma and grandson Raymond, the rabbit meat was a welcome staple at the Atkin's dining table.

The soft, fluffy white fur of the rabbits attracted the boy. He enjoyed petting them. He was drawn to one rabbit in particular, a big doe he called "Bonnie".

Strangely, the rabbit tolerated the little boy and would sit quietly while Raymond ran his tiny hands through her fur.

It was told that if Raymond was to come up missing, he could always be found in Bonnie's hutch, eating alfalfa pellets and quietly communing in boy/bunnie talk.

One Sunday afternoon, the rest of the family came over for dinner and a get together. Rose and Thelma's other sister, Flossie, her husband Ken and their son, Junior were present. Raymond's Uncle Joe and his wife rounded out the family circle.

As Joe was a professional musician, who had one of the first radio shows in the San Francisco Bay Area, he would bring his guitar and sing along with his three sisters.

It wasn't like it is today, with everyone sitting around being entertained by television shows. Everybody got into the act at these parties. Even the kids were encouraged to get up and dance to the lively music.

That particular Sunday had an impact on Raymond that he never forgot. During the dinner, while everyone was gorging on mashed potatoes and gravy, carrots and peas, homemade biscuits and crispy fried rabbit, one unthinking aunt asked, "Does Raymond know that this is his rabbit we are eating?"

Quickly, everyone tried to ease the obvious stress the little boy was experiencing. They tried to tell him on one hand, that it was not his rabbit they were eating and on the other hand chastising Flossie for talking out of turn.

In later years, Raymond wondered what kind of intelligent adult would think that just because a child was of such a young age, he couldn't understand what the people around him were saying. Or, couldn't they understand that a young child could experience deep and painful emotions in response to the conversation?

Steven Sondheim, in his musical play, "Into The Woods" cautions "Careful the things you say, Children will listen...."

MY FIRST CHURCH SERVICE.
ABOUT 1932

Remember, if you will, everything you have ever seen, heard or said still resides in memory. Something you experience may trigger a memory and will push the OPEN button on your mental PC.

I don't recall what brought the thought to mind but as I opened the memory of my first church experience, the pictures of the event came flooding onto my mental screen. I can see flashes, in color, of the people, the sound of the music and the big tent overhead.

It seems like my first time in the house of the Lord was at a revival meeting in San Francisco, in a big tent. I don't know who the preacher was, but I do know the family was really excited about attending this service. About this time there was a big surge of religious fervor in this country. All over the country, preachers toured the states with faith healing services and people flocked to fill the tents they preached within.

Amy Semple McPherson and Billy Sunday were the most widely known preachers of that time. As I say, I do not remember the specifics of that tent meeting, but I do recall the excitement of the crowd. The family had decided to take me with them. I guess it was because there were no such things as baby sitters then and anything the family did, the kids did too. Which even included taking three year old me into a bar to see my Uncle Joe perform on stage. But that is another story.

4

Of all the things that flash into mind, the picture of one man who was pink cheeked and smiling and who was singing along with the congregation. The song, I remember, was "Nothing But The Blood of Jesus". I recall the melody and the words, "What can wash my sins away? Nothing but the blood of Jesus." I recall snatches of the lyrics and snips of the melody and can still hear it in my head. "Oh, precious is the flow, that makes me white as snow." Total recall it is not but hey, it was eighty some years ago. What do you expect?

IMPRISONED

One morning I awakened with a head full of seventy-five year old memories. I don't know whether or not they were the remnants of a dream or just recycled feelings from my childhood.

A rush of memories came in a flood, like running a slide show at rapid speed. Little pictures presented themselves, each with an accompanied emotion. Doctors. Discussions. About me. A long ride in a car. Being left with a lot of strange people. Mother and Dad leaving me with these people. A feeling, in the pit of my stomach, that I would never see my family again. Lost. Alone. Abandoned. Afraid.

My memory of the first day, was, and though not comforting, being put into a room with a few other boys and a Matron. There was bench along one wall and we were instructed to remove all of our clothes and place them on the bench. Modesty forbade doing a strip in front of a member of the opposite sex, but "Matron" informed us not to worry as she had seen lots of little boys without their clothes on and that seemed to make it o.k.

After stripping down we were herded into a large shower and told to soap down, rinse, and dry our selves. Then, we were issued the uniforms we would all wear during our stay at ...Hill Farm.

We soon learned that we were at a facility known as Hill Farm. A real working farm where underprivileged, under nourished children were placed by county authorities to regain a state of health we were evidently lacking.

In uniform of Hill Farm

Both boys and girls, mostly about the same age as I, which as I recall was about six or seven years old, had been sent to Hill Farm. Though we interacted with each other during the day, we were in segregated sleeping quarters. We boys were given cots to sleep on which were situated on an open porch with a large railing around it. We had the benefit of sleeping out in the fresh, night air. We were all issued nightshirts which we boys thought were ankle length dresses.

It was there on that sleeping porch, that I had my break through of acceptance of my situation. I was so terribly homesick that I would awaken in the morning, sobbing, the covers pulled over my head to hide my tears. One morning, one of the boys who's cot was next to mine, told the matron that I was crying. She came to the edge of my bed, pulled the covers down from my face and said, "Raymond, are you crying?" I remember standing on my bed and reaching for her. Tearfully, I blurted out. "I miss my mother." She hugged me and comforted me and let me cry it out. From that point on, I was all right.   In looking back I know I learned that the longer you hold things in, the emotions build to a point where they can no longer be subliminated. Once you let them out, they can no longer make you miserable. The church is aware of this and the confessional or a chat with a minister in confidence, allows one to release things that are hidden and hurting.

Each day found something different to do at Hill Farm.   We went for walks around the farm and saw the crops being cultivated and the dairy where cows provided the milk we would drink. A nice tall glass of cold milk was not an option. The milk we kids drank was only minutes from the cow and still warm from the Bossie's body heat. The milk was served directly from containers that had just come from the dairy and I recall seeing wisps of yellow straw floating on top of the white liquid.

Breakfast was some sort of hot cereal which I tolerated but the slices of raisin nut bread, baked in perfectly round loaves is still something I recall as being absolutely delicious and which I wish I could find today.

Although most of the kids went to classes daily, I don't believe I was ever assigned to a schoolroom and I wandered around during the day chasing lizards and marveling how when grabbed by the tail they would disjoint it and escape to grow another one.

There were sunflowers galore on the farm and we were taught how to remove the seeds from the blossoms and shell and eat them. I have learned that today, health food stores get a pretty penny for a pound of Sunflower seeds that I used to pick for free.

One of my outstanding memories was of a little walk the matrons took us on to view the dead horse. All of the kids were excited because none of us had seen a dead horse before. I remember seeing horses pulling wagons on the streets in front of our houses with the drivers delivering ice for our "ice boxes", (No refrigerators around as yet), or the junk man picking up peoples' cast off items to refurbish and re-sell. Today, old toasters or radios aren't worth the saving and are consigned to the garbage dump.

But, back to the dead horse. We were walked down to a lower pasture and soon saw the body of the large brown equine on its side with legs stiff and straight and a lot of flies buzzing around. We walked around it in amazement. We were seeing a dead horse. I remembered my grandfather in his coffin when he died, but this was a dead horse! Wow!

Evenings were spent in a huge living room with a big stone fireplace. We played games and told stories. This was a co-educational time and we did interact with the girls. I found a photograph of myself and a girl of about the same size, which was taken by my mother when she came to visit. The girl and I were clothed in the same uniform of shorts and t-shirt. Identical in color and style, if it weren't for her longer hair it would be hard to tell who was what.

I remember one boy who I grew friendly with over my months at Hill Farm. He was distinguishable, because he had only one arm. He had been climbing on a billboard and fell off but his arm got caught on a protruding nail and his forearm had to be amputated. This was something I had never before seen and was right up there on a level with the dead horse.

A GOOD SKATE

My mother and stepfather each had a good sense of humor. I mean, they could see the funny side of any incident, where any other parent would have nearly killed me for the stunts I pulled as a kid.

When the folks went shopping on a Saturday, they would sometimes leave me at home to watch over my baby brother, Paul. On this instance, they probably should have brought someone in to watch over both of us. When I think back to that one Saturday in 1935 or '36, I think I was a very lucky little six year old to have lived to become seven.

On the very day in question, I had a brilliant idea. I would go skating. I pictured myself zipping along on the ice as I had seen Sonja Henie do in the movies. The fact that I had no ice skates, or for that matter, no ice (being a summer's day in Alameda, California) was a minute problem that could be overcome with a little six year old ingenuity.

It came to me that to skate, one had to have a slick surface upon which to zip along. The kitchen floor was surely level but taking a good run and a slide wasn't zippy enough. To slide one foot and then the other, as Miss Henie did on a frozen pond, one would have to have a very slick surface. A surface that was really slick didn't necessarily require skates, either. A plain pair of shoes would be just dandy if the floor were slippery enough. Hmmm.

I had seen my mother make cakes with flour and

milk and shortening. Ahhh.. shortening! I recalled that Crisco, was some white stuff in a can that you put into cakes or melted in a pan to fry steak or chops. And if I recollected rightly, it was sort of a greasy stuff. What would happen if you put some of that stuff on the soles of your shoes to make them slippery? So you could skate. Like Sonja Henie.

Well, it seemed like a good idea at the time. Getting the Crisco can down from the cupboard, I scooped out a couple of fingers full and spread it on my shoe soles. I tried the alternate gliding strokes and found it worked pretty well. Then I thought it was really the ice that was slick, not the shoes and if I put a larger amount directly on the floor surface, it would work pretty well.

I guess that was what I was doing when the folks walked in. Gliding gracefully back and forth on the kitchen floor, all the time holding onto the kitchen counter top to keep from falling. It was a real blast.

The fact that I had ruined a pair of shoes, used up a can of Crisco and had made a mess my mother had a dickens of a time to clean up, was ultimately over-looked. As I have found in later years as a father, you can't discipline a kid while you are laughing.

My stepfather shook his head back and forth, grinned and merely said "Damned kids", lumping all of us six year olds in the world into one pot.

It was a story that was told time and again when family and friends gathered. Even when I was a grown man the tale would be brought out, dusted off and retold. I guess it was one of those unbelievable instances when the 'kids will be kids' stories are shared as a "Can You Top This?" subject.

I guess I'm sort of glad that my kids didn't take after their father in inventing ways of passing time.

THE DIMINISHING RANGE

A Remembrance of My Father

My Dad's biggest complaint in life was fences. Back in his thirties, when I was a youngster, he would take me through the ranch lands in Sonoma and Mendocino Counties of California and point out the barbed wire fences that split up the rangeland. He'd note that not too long before that time, all the land was open range and a man could ride horseback for hundreds of miles without meeting another human being.

My grandmother once stated that my dad was "Horse Crazy". All his life he loved horses; the factor that prompted him to become a cowboy. One of the last of the real cowboy stock in California, W.J. Toney had horse manure in his veins. He loved the outdoors and passed on that love to me. I did disappoint him by not taking an interest in ranching or equine love.

"WJ", who was christened William James Toney, answered to many names. Never satisfied with the moniker hung on him by his folks, he changed the spelling of Toney to Tonney, Tonnie, Tone' and perhaps others that might have sounded more dramatic than Toney.

Though of an Irish background, his hair was dark and he sported a tan hide that allowed him to brag he about owning some American Indian blood. As for his Christian name, he was called Jim or Jimmie by his mother and siblings, Bill by others and in later years, just plain Jay.

14

No matter what name he went by, W.J. was only happy on the open range. After working as a cowhand on big Sonoma and Mendocino County ranches, he began to feel pinched in by ranchers and farmers who began to fence and cross fence their acreage. Some of the owners got real testy if a neighbor crossed over onto their parcel. Needing to feel free, W.J. took off for the wide open ranges of Montana, where he worked for a time in logging camps and ranches.

Yearning for home and family, he returned and took up cowboying amidst the shrinking rangelands of northern California. A short lived marriage produced one son.

In the early 1940s, he joined a construction battalion that went to Hawaii to rebuild the facilities at Pearl Harbor after the December 7, 1941 Japanese surprise attack. Sitting on a little south seas island, W.J. felt his ranges were decreasing even further.

After retuning to the mainland, he continued in the construction industry and became a building contractor. He still yearned for the open country and moved north to Mendocino County. He met and married a girl named "Molly"who shared his love of the outdoors and together they purchased a small ranch. They were able to sell the little ranch in Ukiah, California and buy a fourteen hundred acre cattle ranch in Willits. Willits is the northern California town where the famed "Skunk Train" travels across the mountains to the coast.

The Toney spread in Willits, finally became too small when he was known to remark, "We saw chimney smoke over the hill. The neighbors are moving in too close."

Jim and Molly investigated ranchlands afar and soon they purchased a ranch in Arkansas where the land was still vast and thousands of acres could be purchased for a fraction of the cost California real estate prices demanded.

As W. J. and his wife added years to their lives, they developed physical ailments that no longer allowed them to live way out in the boonies. They were forced to move to a small house near downtown Mena, Arkansas. A dog and a cat which they brought with them from the ranch were the only live stock they retained, where once they gazed out over thousands of acres supporting hundreds of head of beef cattle. W.J.s fences were closing in on him and the rangeland was a thing of the past.

As time moved on in its relentless journey to drag a man down into the dust, the ability to ride his beloved horses or rope and hogtie a calf at branding time was beyond him.

Molly's brother lived in southern California and he wanted his sister to be near at hand in case W.J.s failing heart gave out. The Toneys purchased a small cottage in Seal Beach's Leisure World retirement community. Their home was just a few minutes from Long Beach, the permanent berth of the HMS Queen Mary. After a lifetime of freely sailing the oceans of the world, the old ship had been confined to a small inlet at Long Beach as a tourist attraction.

W. J. Toney

How very much alike, the stories of ship and man. Here was the great HMS Queen Mary, no longer able to awaken to clear, new day with nothing around her but blue sea and sky and all the time in the world to sail through them.

And of course, W.J. Toney, a dry land counterpart of the Queen Mary, no longer able to arise to a new day and gaze out over acres of lush, green grass. No longer able to saddle up and ride for days on end.

In his late eighties, W.J. 's body only allows him to walk a short distance before he must sit and rest a while. He arises in the morning to see hundreds of little homes, much like his own. The only blades of grass are a small lawn in the front of the house. The rangelands he once roamed have been pinched in upon him until his boundaries will become a chair, a bed.....?

The hope we have for him is that one day those boundaries will be released, the fences will be torn down and W.J. or Jimmie, or Bill or whatever he will want to be called, will find himself with plenty of open range land and a pretty little sorrel mare to carry him on as far as he wants to ride.

Footnote: The rangeland opened up for William James Toney on February 12, 1993 at 10:45 a.m.

BRISBANE, CALIFORNIA

Part One

About an hour's drive south from San Francisco, Freeway 101 leads you to what is now known as "Silicon Valley". Located in the Santa Clara Valley it is comprised of several cities like San Jose, Sunnyvale, Mountain View, Santa Clara and others where the great electronics industries supplanted the bountiful farms and orchards which had supplied produce to the nation and the world.

In between San Francisco and Silicon Valley, a string of small towns form the area known as "The Peninsula". Along a fifty mile strip of the famous El Camino Real, you'll find Redwood City (Climate Best By Government Test), San Carlos, Belmont and Burlingame. You will also find Menlo Park, Los Altos and Palo Alto, where Leland Stanford founded the University named after him.

At the high end of the financial spectrum, the towns of Atherton and Hillsborough boasted among their citizenry, the Shirley Temple Black and Bing Crosby families. I bring this up to compare with the low end of the totem pole, the town of Brisbane. Brisbane's citizenry included the Rivera, Firth, Hite, Grimes, Felton, Bratton and Campion families among other not so notables.

This small town was situated in the bowl of an extinct volcano and was protected on three sides by the mountain and open on the fourth side to the San

Francisco Bay. Brisbane's weather was usually warm and sunny without the curse of the heavy winds that blew constantly around Belmont to the   south. Fog from the ocean hung up on the surrounding mountains socking in Daly City and Colma but without the lift to get into Brisbane.

Left to right: Mary, Beatrice, "Shaggy", Ray Toney & Jeff

BRISBANE SCHOOL—CLASS OF 1939

Had it been planned properly, Brisbane could have been a millionaire's paradise. Instead, its haphazard development of tiny lots and slap dash construction hardly qualified it to be a slum.

Yet, in my tenth year, Brisbane became home to my mother, Thelma, my step-father Emmett Campion, my brother Paul and of course, little old me. For many low-income families, Brisbane offered the opportunity for home ownership that was not afforded in other, more prosperous locations.

The first home we occupied in Brisbane was a converted old school house. Adjacent to our house was the Catholic Church. And I do mean adjacent. I don't think you could have inserted a playing card on edge between the two buildings. My brother and I had adjoining rooms, which were situated on the church side of the house. Each room was about five feet wide and seven feet long. Barely large enough to accommodate a small bed and a dresser, our rooms each had a small window, high up on the wall where the builder had constructed an air well in a V shape, to allow air in, but in case of a fire, well, forget it.

Because our house had been a school it was probably the only house in town that had two bathrooms, to facilitate use by both boy and girl students.

Our living room was furnished with a blue velvet chaise lounge; the kind where one end rolled up in a backrest but the other end was just plain flat seating area. Abutting the chaise was our Lo-Fi music system which consisted of a console Victrola record player. It was about four feet tall with a lid that tilted back to expose a turntable and playing head.

21

The playing head was attached to the end of a free swinging arm and had a steel needle which fit into the grooves of the 78 rpm records. Two hinged doors on the front could be opened to increase the volume of the music played.

Alongside the turntable was a small metal clasp, which held an object similar to the crank on a model T Ford, only smaller. This crank was inserted into a small hole in the side of the console and was turned to wind up the spring that ran the turntable to produce the sound of the music. I know it sounds kind of complicated to those who are used to CD's and audio tapes.

It could be a challenge at times. Like the fellow who keeps the plates spinning on slender wands, one would have to jump up and go crank like the dickens if the spring wound down during the playing of a record. When you heard the soprano's voice start to slow down and begin to sound like a bass-baritone, you knew it was time to wind up the spring and get her back in key.

Another good thing about the old Victrola, situated like it was at the end of the chaise, when the lid was closed down, it was great fun to climb up on top of it and practice parachute jumps onto the sofa. Obviously our parents' were not aware of this game, or we may not have been able to sit down to eat dinner.

On the other side of the old school house was a small cottage. Andy Ducker, a bachelor, maintained his digs there, accompanied by a small brown terrier appropriately named, "Brownie.

As there were few fences and lots of roaming dogs in Brisbane, Brownie became "known", in the biblical sense, and it was soon evident that Andy's family was about to have several additions. This was exciting to brother Paul and me because Andy had said we could have our picks of the litter.

Evidently Brownie had known several breeds and non-breeds of romantically inclined male dogs because the litter looked like a gathering of totally unrelated pups. Paul and I selected two of the seven available. A small brown dog with a white tip of a tail became Tippy, while the reddish, bull headed one with the black tongue we called, fittingly, Chow.

Chow offered up lots of laughs when it was his dinner time. His overlarge Chow dog head, would overbalance his rear end and while dipping his nose into the food bowl, his hind legs would come up off the floor with his forelegs as a fulcrum point.

As in some communities, there are those people who not only do not like dogs, but go out of their way to destroy them. Such a person was setting out poison for our dog population of Brisbane. Unfortunately not only were Tippy and Chow targets for the poisoner, but their mother, Brownie, received a lethal dose of cyanide on the same day.

Brownie was neighbor Andy's good friend and companion and it was a cruel blow to him to lose her in such a way. Andy had me load the bodies of Tippy, Brownie and Chow onto my wagon and take them to the marsh and bury them. It was a chore he had no heart to do.

A few years later we moved into a larger home on San Benito Way. A local real estate broker, who owned several houses, suggested to my folks that they should get started in home ownership. He arranged for them to take title to the property and carried the note at a reasonable interest rate. It was an early in life lesson to me to always own a home instead of renting. It has been a lesson that stuck with me and I have never rented my personal residence when I could buy. It is the only way I was able to get ahead financially beyond salaried positions.

THE BRISBANE "FLEA HOUSE"
Part Two

Brisbane had one movie theater. Saturday afternoons were the time all the kids in town went to see a movie and thrilled to each weekly episode of the "serials". Buck Jones, Flash Gordon and so many others held us in our seats as they battled the bad guys, only to get blown up or driven off a cliff in a stagecoach or car in the final seconds of the week's episode. You could hardly wait until the following Saturday to find out how the hero got out of the predicament we last saw. Strangely enough, there was always a slightly different version the following week showing the main character jumping out of the careening vehicle just before it went to its doom.

The movie projectionist was a local fellow named "Porky" Hatch. When ever the film would break or the sound would go out of "sync", which was not unusual in those times, every voice in the house would start shouting "Hey, Porky" and keep yelling at him until the problem was fixed and the audience could go back to watching the film.

In those days, candy, popcorn or soft drinks were not offered in the lobby of the theater, so each patron, would stop first at a candy store, to fortify themselves for the double feature.

BRISBANE
Part Three

GLORY, GLORY, HALLELUJAH

Mom and Dad always saw to it that we had our religious upbringing. On Sunday morning, Mom would give us each a ten cent piece for the collection plate and send us off to the local house of God. It never entered my mind that they never came along or took us to church. They didn't join us for classes at Brisbane Elementary School, so why should they come along to Sunday school.

I'm afraid my ten year old mind was a little devious in figuring out a scheme where the collection plate would receive a nickel and the candy store man would share equally in the dime that was intended for the offering. I don't remember if my conscience bothered me for short changing the Lord, but I am sure that if it did, my sweet tooth overcame any shame.

BRISBANE
Part Four

HONOR SATISFIED

Today's macho young men will take umbrage at being "dissed", a shortened version of being disrespected or being disparaged in some way. I assure you though it was not expressed in that manner, Brisbane boys were quick to be angered at some imagined slight and demand "satisfaction".

My good playmate, Virgil Miller, was a cocky little kid who squealed on me after I had soaped a neighbor's car windows and naturally, I took a dim view of that and called him out. We were standing toe to toe about to slug it out when a carpenter working on a new house broke it up and made me walk several blocks out of my way to go home, even though I only lived across the street.

I tried to explain that I lived right there but he wouldn't listen and made me take a hike. About the time I arrived home, my Uncle Joe came home from work and I told him what the carpenter had made me do. Joe called the carpenter over and "dissed" him something terrible, but the carpenter just bobbed his Adam's apple up and down and said he was just trying to keep peace in the neighborhood. Uncle Joe was a good-natured guy and a fine musician but also a pretty big man and not one to mess with.

Settling a matter of honor was mostly a guy thing and quite often one of the boys would challenge another to meet him in a vacant lot after school. Something like duelists, agreeing on a site to commit mayhem on one another.

But the most outstanding after school fight Brisbane ever experienced, was between two seventh graders. A fairly new student, named Don, was challenged by a girl named Lucy. I don't recall what started the ruckus but Lucy insisted on having it out in a traditional Marquis of Queensbury bout.

This was a shocker to all the kids, as never before had a girl invaded the strictly manly art of fisticuffs. Goaded on by their classmates, Don and Lucy met in a vacant lot near the schoolyard. Even though Don kept insisting, as he had been taught, that it wasn't right to hit girls, Lucy attacked and bore in, fists swinging. Don backed off, trying to defend himself without punching Lucy out but was taking a hell of a beating. In desperation, nostrils oozing a bright red, Don took a swing and landed a right cross to Lucy's burgeoning bosom, ending the bout. Of course it was an unpopular decision. As everyone knows you should not hit a girl, but most of all, you do not hit them on their bosom.

BRISBANE
Part Five

THE ALL VOLUNTEER FIRE DEPARTMENT

Brisbane, being unincorporated, did not have the usual police and fire departments. In the event of an unlawful action, the San Mateo County Sheriff's Department answered the call but in the event of a fire, the siren at the firehouse would start wailing and men in cars and pickup trucks from all over town would race to the station where the one fire engine was garaged.

Mostly it was grass fires to be put out but one morning early, at the sound of the siren, we looked out our front window to see the Wilson's house, directly across the street, spouting smoke and flames. Fortunately no one was injured but it did make the house uninhabitable and the Wilson family was forced to move.

BRISBANE
Part Six

MAKESHIFT TOBAGGONING

The hilly configuration of our town allowed for a sporting event that would be the envy of any Norwegian bobsledder.

In the summer, as the warm sunny days turned the waist high green grasses into a California gold color, every boy in town would head for the local grocery store or market to beg for the emptied cardboard boxes that had carried canned goods.

Each boy would drag his cardboard box to the top of one of the steep, grassy slopes. If you pulled the glued sections apart you would wind up with a long strip of tan cardboard. By sitting on one end of the strip and grasping the other end you could pull it back over your feet, just like the curved forward end of a sled. A little scoot and you were flying down the hill lickety-split. Sometimes a hidden rock or two would add a bruise to your backside as you slid over the now flattened grass.

THE RADIO SERIALS

There were no television sets or computers to keep a kid indoors for hours. It was up to us to make our fun and exercise. But there were radios. Every evening before dinner it was time to flop on the floor and listen to the kid's serialized radio shows like "Little Orphan Annie", "The Adventures of Jack Armstrong, The All American Boy" or "Tom Mix and his wonder horse Tony". Tom Mix was a special hero of mine, after my mother told me that before she was married, she used to date 'Curly' Bradley, the actor who played the part of Tom Mix on radio.

Radio was a particularly important to the family as a whole. After dinner we would all gather round and listen to the evening shows like "The Green Hornet" or "Gang Busters" which were exciting adventure series. On Sunday evenings the comedy shows with Jack Benny, featuring Mary Livingston, Phil Harris, Eddie 'Rochester' Anderson, and lots of characters portrayed by Mel Blanc. After the Benny show followed Fred Allen, with Portland Hoffa. I remember their trips down "Allen's Alley", where they met characters like Senator Foghorn.

Our radio was not just any old common tabletop Philco. My step-father was always getting talked into buying, shall we say, different items and our radio was a majestic piece of wonder. It had started out in its state of being as a Juke Box. The insides had been gutted and a radio had been inserted into the bottom half. The top half opened up to reveal a liquor bar with holes of varied sizes cut into the flocked base to hold booze bottles, glasses and an ice bucket. The whole of the thing looked exactly like a jukebox of the day with colorful backlit plastic panels. All in all, it was not the Architectural Digest's idea of good decoration, but to us it was a marvel.

Radio also gave us an awakening jolt on Sunday morning December 7, 1941 as we listened to the news that brought our nation into a full-fledged war with Japan. The bombing of Pearl Harbor, as we heard our President Franklin D. Roosevelt describe as, "A day that will live in infamy".

GEAR UP FOR WAR

The war, as it touched us in Brisbane, brought a lot of changes. All of our windows had to be equipped with blackout shades. During an alert, loud sirens would wail and all lights would be turned off. We would stand outside and watch the searchlights play over the sky looking for enemy bombers. We knew the Japanese were out there somewhere. Their submarines had shelled several of our coastal towns and sunk heavily laden Liberty Ships.

Every man was required to sign up for the draft, a system that categorized men according to their age, physical condition and work or scholastic status. The most eligible for induction, into the armed forces were classified 1-A, the least capable were 4-F.

Men and older boys whom we had known as neighbors, either enlisted or were drafted into the army or navy. Their families proudly displayed a small banner with a blue star in the front window of their home. Sometimes the blue star was taken out of the window and replaced with a gold star. We knew that one of our friends and neighbors had paid the ultimate price and would not be returning to Brisbane ever again.

Our local shipyards and steel manufacturing plants employed many of our Brisbane men and women who went into "War Work".

My future father in law, Harold Mack, had been performing at the Golden Gate Theater in San Francisco when war broke out. He gave up a headlining act on the vaudeville circuit and became an insulation installer working on new ships under construction. He moved his family into a mobile home park, (then called trailer parks), in Brisbane and helped in the war effort. Unfortunately the insulation material most used in those days was asbestos. No one knew the dangers of working with asbestos fibers at that time. It ultimately shortened his life and career on the stage. After the war was over, he took his daughter, Barbara and his father, Robbie on tour in an act called Three Generations. It was shortly after that that I was introduced to his daughter and my wife to be.

My introduction to my future wife, was made by the local dance and music teacher in Brisbane. Bunnie Phipps had been a touring musician with an all girl band, when she met and married Gene Firth, a drummer in another band. It was a romance of note, one might say. Bunnie had a large dance studio and one day when I was visiting her, Barbara Mack, who had just returned from a nation wide tour of theaters and television shows, came by and we met and hit it off pretty well. But, that's another story of a later day.

31

Back to childhood in Brisbane, two of our class-mates were Johnny Rivera and Lucy Gomez. They were the first Mexican kids I had ever known. Johnnie's family raised goats, which were staked out to feed in the meadow next to the Rivera house. One day I noticed that one of the little goats was missing and I asked Johnnie at school what had happened to it. He explained that the family had a fiesta and had slaughtered the kid to roast for the family feast. It set me back a little bit but then I recalled that my grand-father had raised rabbits, which were a part of our staples when I was very young.

Another aside: When I was a toddler, in my grandparent's yard, there was a big New Zealand White doe that was my pet. They say that if I came up missing, they could always find me in the doe's hutch. I have a picture taken of me at about one year old with the rabbit by my side. One day, they had a bunch of relatives in for a big dinner and I recall rab-bit was the main course. One of my aunt's spoke in a hushed voice, "Do you suppose Raymond knows that it is his rabbit we are eating?" Even at that young age, my heart sank Believe it, even the smallest of children can understand what adults are saying so take care what comes out of your mouths where they little ones are concerned.

Bunnie Firth, the music teacher, was my brother Paul's piano teacher. Every year she would have her recital in the local Brisbane Theater. One year, Paul's recital piece was "Little Brown Bear" which he polished off very well for a six year old. He later switched to trumpet which turned out to be his lucky choice and which he still played very well until his passing at the age of seventy-six from heart failure.

As I noted, Bunnie Firth was the local music teacher who taught piano, brass and reeds but a dance teacher named Carol suggested a joint venture to be called the Bunnie Carol Studio for Music and Dance. The only problem was that Carol took in the month's advance receipts and left town. This left Bunnie with the necessity of teaching dance, as well as music. Not having the money to refund what Carol had absconded with, Bunnie would run into San Francisco to a dance studio there, take a lesson and run back to her studio to teach the same material to her newly acquired dance pupils. She kept ahead of the class by one lesson but in due time became proficient enough to open several dance school locations.

One of Bunnie's sons, Eugene Firth Jr., was a wizard musician who at the age of four picked up a trumpet and played a popular tune of the day called "Sweet Lorraine". Some how the boy also picked up the nickname of "PUZZY".

Puzzy was a little demon and true to Brisbane form he drove everyone nuts with his antics. One afternoon when his mother came home she couldn't find the family cat and asked Puzzy if he knew where it was. He claimed he didn't know but when it was time to make dinner, Bunnie opened the refrigerator and there amid every kind of food and condiment was a dead cat who had trashed the entire contents of the frig trying to get out.

Puzzy took up his father's instrument and became a drummer. During the war years Bunnie put together a group of Brisbane kids who were students of hers and formed an entertainment group to tour the army camps in the Bay Area. She aptly named them "The Demoralizers" a great name for a group trying to lift the spirits of soldiers far from home. She dressed Puzzy in a Superman costume befitting his five year old frame and he played a wild set of drums to a swing tune of the forties.

In keeping with the "local boy makes good" theme, Puzz Firth became the bass player with the Vince Guaraldi combo and was featured on all of the Peanuts recordings from the "You're a Good Man Charlie Brown" movie, based on Charles Schultz' characters.

BRISBUS

The only mode of transportation in and out of Brisbane was the family car. I say "the" family car because folks in the 1930's were lucky to have one car let alone two. So a man named Curtis Richards started a bus company to provide service to the outside world. The little bus's riders gave it the sobriquet "BRISBUS" by which it was known to all the town folk.

BRISBUS was my weekly transportation to my music teacher's studio. At least it took me within a mile of my destination. I would board BRISBUS with my trusty violin case and ride from Brisbane along Bayshore Highway to a little settlement called Bayshore City. I would get off the bus at Geneva Ave. and walk from there to Schwerin Street, which to me, wasn't just a street, it was the Matterhorn. From the bottom of the hill you could look up Schwerin Street to the very top where my music teacher, Mr. Kessen, lived and had his studio. After climbing to the top of this pinnacle without benefit of ropes and pitons, I would spend an hour learning correct bowing techniques and positions. (My stepfather complained that after all the music lessons my forte was imitating Jack Benny playing Love In Bloom). Badly.

After my music lesson, I would walk down Schwerin Street, which was much easier than going up, and retrace my steps beside the PG&E substation on Geneva Ave. to Bayshore Highway, where I would wait until the BRISBUS came along to return my tired body home. I often quip that I had to give up my violin lessons because my legs gave out.

Curtis Richards had a daughter named Doris. Doris was one of my playmates and we went through elementary and high school together. I lost track of her after high school but still admit I was smitten with the young lady. One day, while I was plighting my troth, as ten year olds are wont to do, Doris began throwing rocks at me and after getting hit on the head, I retreated with the thought that she must love me to go to so much trouble.

A kid I used to play with was into rocket ships and sword fighting. I often wondered what became of Bobby as he would have fit right in with the astronaut program and the scientists of the space age.

Bobby Gregory had his own playhouse on the hill behind his parents' home. The playhouse, which wasn't much more than an old chicken house, had a big plate glass window looking out over the top of his folks' residence. This became the front window of our space ship. We built flight controls on the tabletop beneath the window and assumed character names. He was "Speed" and I was "Dynamite". Upon landing on some far away planet, we would find a way to get into wood lath sword fights. As we had no alien creatures to battle, we would wind up fighting each other with our pine slat epees. I was very proud when Bobby told me he thought I was one of the best sword fighters he had ever been matched against.

At Brisbane school, I got my first job. I worked in the cafeteria cleaning up tables after lunch. The Brisbane Elementary School had varied menus that were repeated every week. The Monday meal was a hot dog, the fare for a Tuesday would be macaroni and cheese, and so on. My compensation for cleaning up was my lunch at no cost. Unfortunately I was out of school with a bad cold for two weeks and when I returned, I found they had replaced me with someone who could be available to work. Another valuable lesson learned. The only reason you don't show up for work is if you are at a funeral and the funeral is your own.

Eighth grade was as high as one could attain at Brisbane School. From there on you became a freshman at Jefferson Union High School in Daly City, a forty minute bus ride away. In 1943 we were bussed and didn't think anything of it.

MAY I HAVE THIS DANCE?

In addition to our regular eighth grade studies,

social graces became a requirement. We would have Friday afternoon dances where all the boys and girls dressed a little fancier and we would learn how to ask a girl how to dance, "May I have the honor of this dance?" Or how to accept graciously, if one was a girl responding. "Why of course, and thank you for asking."

The final dance was just before graduation and everyone attended in his best finery. The girls were coiffed and frocked and the boys had their hair slicked back and wore ties with their white shirts. At this time, all of our teachers were women. I don't recall ever having a male teacher in elementary school. I never had a man teacher until high school, which is far different than in this current age where men can be found teaching the primary grades.

The women teachers from all the grades were present for that last dance. I guess I must have cut a fine figure doing my side together, side together two step. I had just finished dancing with a gangly eighth grade girl and properly returned her to her seat when one of the teachers, probably in her early twenties, (and quite attractive), said to me "Are you going to ask me to dance?" I was a little taken aback but in a quite courtly manner, bowed slightly and performed the ritual of asking obsequiously, if the lady would like to have "this dance".

In looking back, I am sure this was a spur of the minute attempt at "having a little fun with the kid". I led the young teacher onto the dance floor and as the music started, I placed my right hand on her waist and took her right hand in my left and began to lead her across the floor to rhythm of the recorded slow ballad. "Can't get out of this mood, can't get over this feeling", the vocalist sang plaintively. All of a sudden, to my complete surprise, the left hand of my partner, which had started out on my right shoulder suddenly encircled my neck and drew me close up tight to her. I found myself hip to thigh and chest to breast with this very pretty twenty something woman.

I know now she was just having a bit of teasing fun, however my physical reaction I am sure was just what you would expect from a thirteen year old lad in such a situation. I don't even remember the rest of the dance, only that I was glad to finish it and bow out and turn and walk away quickly. But it was a memorable conclusion to the Brisbane Elementary School Eighth Grade Dance.

TRICK OR TREAT

Halloween in Brisbane was a big event. As most kids in a small town, we figured out ways of tricking that were beyond the simple soaping of windows. One of my Trick or Treat buddies, Henry Miller, suggested we set a paper bag on fire on a man's porch and then run like hell. We got some fresh dog poop and put it in a paper bag. We then twisted the top of the bag into a fuse and lit it. Then we rang his doorbell and ran off.

The whole idea was that the victim, seeing the burning bag on his porch was supposed to stamp on it to put out the fire, thereby mushing his shoes into the dog poop. The only problem was that the neighbor didn't stop to stomp the bag but just took out after us.

We ran like the devil was after us and would have got away except that Henry grabbed me and stopped us while the enraged man proceeded to vilify us and our ancestry going way, way back.

After he had vented his ire, the man turned and walked back to his house. I asked Henry, "Why did you stop us? We could have got away." My co-trickster just said, "Oh, I just wanted to see what he was going to say."

That wasn't the only time Henry got me into the doghouse. He once suggested that we pepper his grandmother's trailer house with our BB guns. Late one night we lay in the grass and sniped away leaving several pits in a window. That little episode cost my folks five dollars for a new window. In the thirties, five dollars was a lot of money. As the man said, "It seemed like a good idea at the time."

VENTURE PARTNERS

I went into business with Henry Miller and learned another lesson. You cannot buy a dollar's worth of penny candy at retail from the corner grocery, set up a stand and sell it for the same price you paid for it. Considering the investment was all mine and considering that Henry helped me eat the stock it turned out to be a bad investment. To this day I will not go into business with any one named Henry.

Johnnie Randrup and I used to go to Phil's Fountain on San Benito Way whenever we got a few cents ahead. We would order a Tulip Sundae with chocolate, vanilla and strawberry ice cream, covered with chocolate syrup, pineapple topping, whipped cream, marshmallow, nuts and a cherry. Phil would make up these concoctions at our direction and I think we blew the whole bankroll on one of these confections.

It just so happened that Phil needed someone to help clean up around the fountain and he hired us to do the job and paid us a salary the equivalent of the cost of one of our sundaes. It was a pretty good deal for Phil, for we would belly up to the fountain and spend our whole pay on a triple Tulip Sundae. As soon as Phil paid us for our labor, it went right back over the counter into his cash register.

SHOPPING WITH MOM

During the war, we were issued ration books with stamps and small tokens. When we would go to the store to buy groceries or meat, we would have to surrender a certain number of stamps or tokens along with the price of the item. The market was probably a mile away from our house and as we had no transportation, our mom would make a daily journey for our food. I was usually asked to go along with her and help carry the bags.

Today's meat markets with their pre-packaged cuts are so different than the markets of the forties. We knew the butcher by name and he knew our entire family and when we shopped for hamburger or chops, he would reach into the meat display case and pull out a wiener as a gift for each of the kids. Funny how good a cold hot dog tasted right out of the case.

Mom used to kid the butcher by telling him to keep his thumb off the scale when he was weighing her purchases. The both of them would laugh but I don't know how many of the butcher's thumbs we paid for.

A large beef knuckle bone that today's market packages and sells for $1.99 a pound, was wrapped up in butcher paper as a treat for the family dog, at no cost. Our German Shepherd dog, Pal, was very well behaved. He would wait outside the market and when we appeared, ready to go back home, he would be given his bone package to carry. He would never try to open it and would pick it up in his mouth and walk all the way home with it. Only after he was told "O.K. Pal" would he rip off the paper and start gnawing away.

At this time, the family actually had two dogs, the aforementioned German Shepherd and a little black and white Border Collie of mixed heritage. Due to his fluffy coat, we kids gave him the name Shaggy. Shaggy was always getting Pal into trouble. If a stray dog entered the neighborhood, Shaggy would run up to it barking and snarling and just when the other dog began to get testy, Shaggy would run over to his big brother, Pal and stand under him, looking out from between his forelegs. Then the two would chase the intruder away.

Pal actually belonged to our Uncle Joe, my mother's brother who, when he found a place where he could have a dog, took Pal to live with him. We missed our old Pal but were very proud to hear that he had joined the police force of a small San Joaquin valley town and aided in capturing desperados.

Little Shaggy was always getting into trouble. One Sunday afternoon, after our usual mid afternoon dinner, the family left the table to go into the living room to listen to one of the top radio shows. Instead of cleaning up the table right away, our mother didn't want to miss any of the beginning of the show. At the first commercial break, she went into the kitchen and let out a loud shriek. We all jumped up to see what the problem was and there was Shaggy under the stove chewing on the rest of our roast beef dinner. The temptation was too great. Smelling that meat, he climbed up on a chair and then onto the table and dragged off about a pound and a half of beef that would have been sandwiches for all of our Monday bag lunches.

INTRODUCTION TO SHOW BIZ

The stage of the Brisbane Theater was my introduction into performing before several hundred people.

The aforementioned Bunnie Firth had put together a group of young singers, dancers and musicians to perform for the USO and bay area army and navy camps. Every variety show should have a master of ceremonies to introduce the acts and Bunnie, decided that I would be our spokesman.

Having spent a good deal of time in the front row of San Francisco's Golden Gate Theater, I had the opportunity to watch classic performers on that marvelous, huge stage. My cousin, Ken Hanson and I used to take the bus into San Francisco every Saturday morning and head directly to the Golden Gate. We would arrive about the time the box office opened and after buying our tickets we would head for the first row, right up against the orchestra pit. With necks craned back and eyes tilted nearly skyward, we would watch the filmed Previews of Coming Attractions, cartoon and the news reel and of course the feature film.

Stand-up at the Brisbane Theater

No matter how uncomfortable that viewing position was, it was worth the neck strain to be up close and personal as the great performers of the day did their "turn" on stage. Great stars appeared and sang, danced and told jokes to an appreciative audience. I was fortunate to see fabulous talents as Danny Kaye, The Mills Brothers, Eddie Cantor, Frank Sinatra, Judy Garland, Bill Robinson and the Big Bands of Lionel Hampton, Spike Jones, Count Basie, Benny Goodman and Artie Shaw among the many who toured in those days. Of course, we would sit through the movie all over again just to see the stage show the second (and sometimes third) time through.

I watched the M.C.'s and learned how to properly introduce an act and keep the show going, with jokes interspersed between the introductions. I listened for audience reaction and learned how to time a punch line for the biggest laugh. These lessons were my instruction into becoming the Master of Ceremonies for the Demoralizers at the Brisbane Theater. We would travel into San Francisco with our little troupe to the USO club on lower Market Street and entertain the members of the armed forces who were far from home and were the greatest audience in the world.

I will always be grateful to Bunnie Firth for giving me the opportunity to stand up in front of hundreds or later, thousands of people and command their attention. And get laughs besides.

WE MOVE ON

Farewell To Brisbane

We spent a lot of time and learned a lot in Brisbane, California. But as time goes by and opportunity arises, families move on. As I was now attending Jefferson Union High School in Daly City, California and as Dad Campion had moved up in the employment world, we moved to a more convenient and more up scale neighborhood.

Our new home on Winchester Street in Daly City would provide the base from which Mother was able to get involved in social and service activities. She joined the Eastern Star and rose to be Worthy Matron of her chapter. Dad Campion joined the Masonic Order as did brother Paul later in life.

After a term at The College of San Mateo, I chose to join the U.S. Army to get my service commitment over with. My good friend Bob Statton enlisted at the same time and we went overseas together.

But my time in Brisbane, will always be a special time of my life.

A MOUSE IN THE HOUSE...

Or.....I Smell A Rat...

The family spent almost every weekend at our cabin on Sandmound Slough, a small offshoot of the San Joaquin River, in northern California. The area was fairly remote and the property could only be reached by driving on a dirt road for the last few miles.

The cabin sat on a flat piece of land protected from flooding by a levee, which surrounded the thousands of acres of farm and recreation land. On the river side of the levee, my step father had built a small dock to which was tied a little 22′ cabin cruiser which was used for fishing trips or short cruises.

On Sunday evening, we would drive back to San Francisco to begin another week of work for Dad and school for my brother Paul and me. Mondays Mom would launder all the dirty clothes and sheets from the weekend trip and get her housework done.

On one particular Monday, my mother opened the vegetable bin and noticed that some of the potatoes had little scratches on them as though something had been nibbling at them. She saw nothing else out of the ordinary and forgot about it.

About noon, Mother opened a can of Campbell's Tomato Soup for her lunch and holding the opened can in her right hand, she opened the drawer in the stove, which contained pots and pans, with her left. As she reached for a small pot, a rat, which had somehow taken up residence in that drawer, jumped out of the pot directly at her.

I suppose that it was a frightening situation for both the rat and my mother. The rat scampered around the floor of the kitchen looking for an escape route. With a scream, to rival any Hollywood starlet faced with her first glimpse of the Frankenstein monster, Mom threw up her hands and leapt for the nearest chair.

The fact that she had an open can of tomato soup in hand was not even considered in the heat of the moment. Tomato soup splattered the walls, the floor and even the ceiling. The now empty can rolled round on the floor and finally ended up under the stove, leaving a trail of red in its wake.

When I got home from school, my mother and little brother Paul, were waiting in the dining room. The doors to the kitchen were closed tightly to keep the intruder locked in. It seems it was up to me to dispatch the furry little rodent although my younger brother was ready and willing to join in the battle.

Grabbing a broom, I eased into the kitchen and started poking around behind the refrigerator and the stove. A switch of the broomstick, under the firebox of the stove, brought results and the little creature zoomed out and headed for the nearest doorway.

Finding his exit barred by the closed and latched door Mr. (or Mrs.) Rat launched himself (or herself) at the door, leaping to doorknob height in a single bound. (apologies to Siegel and Shuster).

My brother Paul, in the meantime, had gone into my room and removed the Civil War cavalry saber I had hanging over my bed, and taking a mighty swing at the rat, he managed to take a two inch gouge out of the door panel. Thankfully he missed the wayward rodent. I can well imagine the gory sight of a skewered rat in the aftermath of being eviscerated by a Civil War cavalry saber.

After several near misses with the broom, I finally made solid contact and after a few good swats, the story came to a climax.

How the little creature got into the house we never knew but I at least know how he left. Feet first, as they say.

88 REASONS WHY

My son, you probably have wondered why I was so insistent about you attending your piano lessons when you were a kid. I am sorry that I did not realize your teacher was a minor Hitler whose method was not to teach, but to beat, the skill, or art, if you will, of playing the piano, into her students.

It all goes back to the time when I was of a comparable age. Playing the piano was my one true love. My folks paid for piano lessons and I was doing pretty well. In her annual recital, my teacher selected a piece about flowers or a flower garden, the actual name of which, I cannot remember, for me to perform.

I guess I got through it pretty well as I vaguely remember the applause. Especially that of my mother. Moms are always our biggest fans.

We had a big old upright piano in the living room, (we were too poor to have a parlor). I would sit and practice every day and be all in my glory, as I was improving with each practice session.

One day, the neighborhood kids came over to get me to come out to play with them. I told them I couldn't come out now as I was practicing the piano. "Oh that's sissy stuff". They yelled at me "Go tell your mom you want to quit."

To this day, there is no better lesson I have learned than to let no man, woman, boy or girl convince me to make decisions about my life that could be a detriment to my well being.

Thinking it over, I knew that if I went to my mother and told her I wanted to quit my piano lessons, she would tell me to get back in there and practice my scales.

It was a win, win situation. The guys would know I tried to quit and my mother would say I couldn't stop the lessons and I would get to continue playing my beloved piano.

Figuring it out in my seven year old brain, I went in and told Mother "I want to quit those old piano lessons."

Shock, surprise and anguish hit me in the solar plexus as I heard her reply, "OK. No more piano lessons."

"NO! NO!" I thought. Mothers are supposed to be in charge. She was supposed to say "Get in there and practice that new song." But she didn't! I had asked for something that was the last thing in the world that I really wanted. It was granted without any argument.

I could have spoken up and told her that I really didn't want to quit. I should have told her that I really didn't mean it. It was my pals who wanted me to quit. I really didn't want to lose my opportunity to advance my skills that were improving as I studied.

But even young kids are cursed with a stubborn streak. I had asked for something and it was granted. There was no way I could go back to her and tell her that I loved my piano lessons and that old upright piano. So, I turned and went out to play.

Years later, as I fumble around on the piano with my self-taught skills, I wonder if I could have attained the ability I appreciate in well schooled pianists.

I guess that is why I didn't want to be the parent who said, "All right. You can quit" when down deep it might be something you would regret all your life.

THE GREAT KOREAN
CONFLICT

The Korean War, or as it was known as in that period, a "Police Action", became personal to me when I received an official letter from my Uncle Sam. The letter informed me that as a member of the United States Army Inactive Reserve, I was being called up for active duty.

Having served in the regular army at the end of WWII, I elected, upon separation, to become a member of the "inactive" reserve rather than go to meetings as an active reservist.

The interesting part of this decision became evident at the outbreak of the Korean conflict. We inactive reservists were called to duty while all my friends who became active reservists stayed home and went to meetings.

I quit my regular job, said my goodbyes to friends and family and reported to Ford Ord, California. Fort Ord is a military establishment near Monterey, California and after a few weeks of re-indoctrination and getting supplied with new uniforms and gear, I received orders to be assigned to the 343rd General Hospital at Fort Lewis, in the state of Washington.

Fort Lewis is near the town of Tacoma and south of Seattle. Upon arriving at Ft. Lewis, I was assigned to be a 'fireman'. This was not the kind of fireman who puts out fires, but one who keeps them going.

The barracks were huge two story brick buildings, each building being heated by coal fired furnaces. It was our job as firemen to keep those furnaces putting out heat day and night. Washington was a state not known for its sunny climate and was always overcast or rainy and cold. I don't think that I even had a glimpse of the sun except for one day out of about four months.

Our duty hours were staggered so that we would rotate shifts with each man having twelve hours on and twenty four hours off. On the 8 p.m. to 8 a.m night shift, you could fill up the huge coal hoppers that fed the furnaces and sleep for a few hours on the cot in the furnace room. Then up again shoveling coal into the hoppers.

SEATTLE, WASHINGTON
And Jazz At The Philharmonic

Having twenty-four hours off every other day left plenty of time to see the sights of the Pacific Northwest. Seattle is a city of many faces. Its unique diversity draws a broad range of personalities; the aircraft workers of Boeing, the fishermen and merchant mariners fresh into port from days or weeks upon the sea, the Oriental population of one of the largest Chinatown settlements and of course, the soldier on week-end pass up from Fort Lewis.

As one of the latter, and a jazz fan, I wanted to attend the big Jazz At The Philharmonic concert at the Seattle Civic Auditorium. I dressed up in my best dark blue, one button roll, double breasted suit with the dark blue knit tie affixed around my neck by a

53

huge Windsor knot and headed for the bus station.

In Seattle, I took a short term lease on one of the leading hotel's least expensive rooms, and toured the town afoot. In need of a pair of new shoes, I stopped in at a Nordstrom's department store and settled into a chair in the shoe department.

An attractive, tall, slender black lady took the chair two seats down from mine. While we were waiting for our respective salesmen to find the shoes of our choice in the correct sizes, we struck up a conversation. She said that her name was Alicia and I told her that my target for the evening was the JATP concert at the auditorium. The most famous names in Jazz would be performing; Lester Young, Flip Phillips, Coleman Hawkins, Buddy Rich, Trummy Young and others.

JATP was promoted by a fellow named Norman Granz, the Bill Graham of his day. Alicia said she would love to see it too. Perhaps we would see each other later. I bought my oxblood colored loafers and left to see what else Seattle held in store for a visitor with not a lot of bucks to spare from a private's salary.

After returning to the hotel, I showered alone for the first time in several months and decided to enjoy a touch of bourbon before dinner. The hotel featured a bar called "The Flame Room". I found a stool at the center of the gleaming hardwood bar and glanced at myself in the mirrored back bar.

Sipping my bourbon and ginger, I noted that the glass in which it was served was especially designed to conform to the 'flame' theme of the lounge, with leaping tongues of fire cast right into the goblet's outer wall.

It was at this time I learned never to lift a glass to look at its design with the lights of the back bar gleaming through it. For in raising my glass to look at the flame design, my action was misconstrued as if I were raising my glass in a toast to a natty looking man in his late forties who occupied a stool just around the corner of the bar from where I sat.

With a smile and a flourish, the fellow raised his glass in what he thought was a return salute, and leaving his stool, came around and took the empty seat beside me. Without asking, he ordered the bartender to provide me with an additional drink and plopped a roll of one hundred dollars bills down on the bar.

It seems this well-heeled "Good Samaritan" was a merchant marine who had just arrived in port and was looking for a good time. "There's three thousand dollars there," he said, "and you and I are going to spend it all and have a ball tonight."

At the age of twenty two I had never been propositioned by anyone, man or woman, before. I wasn't sure of what the guy was up to but I said, in my deepest voice, "Sorry, but I've got a date tonight to go to the jazz concert."

"A date? With who?" Thinking quickly I came up with, "A girl I met in a shoe store today."

"A girl? What do you want to go out with a girl for? Break the date. We can have a swell time. I've got three months pay here. You and me, we can have a ball!"

I finished my drink, told a disappointed sailor goodbye and left the lounge, vowing never again to lift a glass off a bar any higher than the bottom of my nose.

The concert was terrific and I taunted myself for not taking up on Alicia's guarded wish to see the concert and asking her to join me. However, after the last note was played and the last bow taken, I turned to walk up the aisle toward the exit and there, pretty as a Powers model and impeccably dressed, was Alicia and a very handsome escort. She smiled and waved at me and I returned the gesture. I could see the question forming in the mind of her friend, but of course, never heard it or the answer.

THE OLD ORLEANS CLUB

Reid Saindon was a fellow reservist who was called back into active service at the same time I was. He had a car which he drove up to Fort Lewis and therefore had personal transportation. He and I would drive up to Seattle or Tacoma for an occasional dinner or a show. Reid was a pilot who later became Chief Pilot for the Hap Harper flying service located on the San Francisco Peninsula.

It was on one of our jaunts to Seattle. We were heading back to Fort Lewis late one night, when we saw a GI standing on a corner looking kind of worse for wear. You might say drunk. Reid thought we should give the guy a ride so we stopped and picked him up. We asked if he knew of a place where we could get a drink that late at night and he directed us to an old part of town in an industrial section.

He instructed us to go up to a building and knock on the door. It was really dark in the area and we walked across the street, leaving the soldier to sleep it off in the back seat of Reid's car.

We knocked on the door and a little peephole opened. An eyeball looked out and a voice asked what we wanted. We told the eye that we just wanted to get a drink and his place was recommended to us by one of his customers. The voice said that they were a private club open to members only. We asked how one became a member and were told that a membership card could be obtained by paying an initiation fee of fifty cents. We agreed to the terms and were invited into a small foyer lit by a single red bulb. After paying our initiation fees we were presented with cards stating that we were official members in good standing of the Old Orleans Club.

We were ushered into a back room with a bar, a dance floor and a jukebox. It was at this time that we noted that there were only two Caucasians in the club. Reid and me. Although this was a black after hours club, we were welcome members of the Old Orleans Club and we made several trips there while we were in Seattle. The people were friendly, the music was good and the drinks were certainly not watered.

HEADING FOR THE FAR EAST

The 343rd General Hospital was a reserve unit from Syracuse, New York and was comprised of doctors, nurses, clerical staff and people like furnace feeders.

The only thing we didn't have was a hospital or

the equipment to run one. The commanding officer was a doctor with a colonel's rank but rank held no particular status in our company. Everyone ate together and it didn't matter who was a private, a sergeant or an officer, when the dinner bell rang everyone lined up on a first come first served basis.

That is, until we arrived in Camp Otsu, just outside Kumagaya, Japan where the hospital building we were to staff was located. Once we got situated, the officers had their own mess hall and NCO's and enlisted men had their's.

Still, we did not have an operational hospital and didn't have too many duties to perform. I was assigned to the hospital newspaper, "Your Mouthpiece" where I started out as a reporter and later was promoted to editor.

The Service Club at the camp was pretty nice and we could go there to be entertained, or just hang out and read or play cards. One evening, during an intermission at a dance at the club, the hostess asked if I would go back to one of the music rooms and ask a Mr. Nesbitt if he would play a few tunes on the piano.

As I approached the music room, I heard some terrific jazz piano being played. I knocked and entered and asked for Mr. Nesbitt who was seated at the piano. He agreed to play for the intermission. This meeting was the beginning of a long term association between Joe Nesbitt, Dick Zappala and me. We spent a couple of years together touring service clubs and hospitals performing the act we put together at Camp Otsu.

We three traveled to Tokyo to audition for a huge,

international stage show to be produced at the Ernie Pyle Theater. The theater, which had been a world class motion picture and variety house before the war, had been taken over by the United States and renamed in honor of a well known and beloved newspaper columnist, who had been killed by sniper fire in the Pacific Theater of Operations. We performed our act for the producers, which was so well accepted, that not only were we booked into the big show, we were slotted in the prized 'next to closing' spot. We were to go back to our respective army units and await orders for transfer to the theater company.

Shortly, we received our TDY (temporary duty) orders and packed up all our gear and headed for Tokyo and our new assignment. On the day we left Camp Otsu for Tokyo, the weather was miserable with snowstorms halting most traffic. Joe, Dick and I were able to get an ambulance and driver from the hospital motor pool and after skidding off the road several times arrived at the railway station at Kumagaya.

We got our tickets and hopped aboard the train for Tokyo. We started out on our adventure with great anticipation. Our excitement lasted about ten minutes as our train ran into snow banks and we had to sit and wait until the tracks were cleared ahead. This became a frustrating occurrence about every 10 to fifteen miles.

Aboard the train, we were joined by Bob Arrelanes, a musician who was being transferred to the Armed Forces Radio Station in Tokyo. Arrelanes had been a staff organist for one of the big radio networks, I believe it was CBS, out of Los Angeles. He was a very talented musician whose professional name was Bob Baron. It was his playing that was heard as the background for soap opera shows like Myrt and Marge, Our Gal Sunday, or Ma Perkins.

The now four of us, filled the time by talking between ourselves or with some of the Japanese citizens aboard the train. One particular Japanese gentleman, who sat directly across from me in the facing seats, offered to share his lunch with me. The meal consisted of rice, seaweed and raw fish and though I thanked him and bowed profusely, I declined, noting that we had just eaten before getting aboard the train.

With my smattering of the Japanese language and an equally limited amount of English on his side, my companion, (I'll call him Watanabe San) and I conversed about the weather "Yuki, dome, ne?" which translated into a pidgin English version of "bad snow storm, no?" or "Gohan oishi?" "is the rice tasty?"

Needless to say this was not exactly passing the time in an intellectual discussion. My American traveling companions, Joe, Dick and Bob were getting about as 'antsy' as I was. Americans do not do delays well. Our patience quota was well used up after a couple of hours of getting absolutely nowhere on the train, so one of us suggested that the next town we came to, we would get off the train and transfer to a bus to travel the rest of the way.

At the next town, we packed up our bags and after saying Sayonara to Watanabe San, we got off the train and looked for a bus station. Seeing none, there was none and as our train had left, we had to seek alternate transportation. This ultimately was resolved as we commandeered an open flat bed truck that was heading for Tokyo with a load of sake, the popular Japanese rice wine.

The weather was foul but at last we were moving towards our goal at a slow but steady pace. The driver of the sake truck said he would take us to the RTO at Ueno where the steam trains unloaded passengers who then took the electric trains into the city. After freezing our butts off, sitting on top of the straw covered sake bottles, we finally arrived at the electric train station and passing the driver a couple of hundred yen, we toted our gear towards the depot.

As we were walking along the sidewalk, we noted all of the people who had just come off the steam trains, and suddenly, I broke into uncontrolled laughter. My buddies tried to get me to tell them what was so funny but I was laughing so hard I couldn't speak for several minutes. When I finally got my laughter under control, I explained that as we were walking towards the depot I came face to face with a very recognizable man. Mr. Watanabe, who had stayed aboard the train in warmth and comfort, had arrived at the exact same time as we, who had elected to leave for a quicker, if colder, method of transportation.

Upon arrival in Tokyo, we slushed through several feet of snow. It was, we were told, the worst snowstorm in thirty some years.

Reporting to the Ernie Pyle Theater, we met our director and non-com in charge, Sergeant Ray Scott Davis. After hearing Ray Scott Davis's gravelly voiced greeting, it was hard to accept that this man had been a fine vocalist. His tenor voice had been shattered by enemy gunfire early in the war. Though his voice had changed drastically, he could still belt out a blues song in the style of Louis 'Satchmo' Armstrong or Jack Teagarden.

The "Emanon Trio"
Ray, Dick Zapalla, Joe Nesbitt, in the Green Room

As we met the other performers for the show we found we were in very good company. Andrea Daikovich, a dancing star of Hungarian motion pictures was featured along with American baritone Arlington Rollman, in a big production number based on the play South Pacific. Norbert d'Coteau, a fine classical pianist, trained at the famed Juilliard School of music, was among others in the cast.

Arlington Rollman was a big, blond, man with a booming voice who was a star with Japan's Fujiwara

Opera Company, one of the world's finest. His story was sort of sad as well as interesting. Arlington's theatrical agent had two possibilities lined up for him. He had auditioned and been offered two jobs. The first was a tour of the Philippine Islands and Japan with the aforementioned Fujiwara Opera Company, or the second option was the second lead in a new musical play to open on Broadway about World War II, as fought in the Pacific Theater of Operations.

Believing no one would want to see a play about war, after just experiencing the real thing, Arlington elected to take the tour with the world class opera company. The role he turned down, was accepted by Italian singer Ezio Pinza. The show was South Pacific, starring Mary Martin.

Joe, Dick, Betty Lehman, Ray

While rehearsing for the big show at the Ernie Pyle, we were approached by a booking agent who offered us the opportunity to do casuals at various NCO and Officer's Clubs. We put together a shortened version of our act and started entertaining three or four nights a week. We were in demand and pretty soon we were making far more money than our army pay. For close to a year while on TDY we rarely ate in military dining halls but would eat in some of the finer restaurants in the Tokyo/Yokohama area. Instead of traveling by train to go forty or fifty miles, we took taxicabs.

Rehearsals for the Ernie Pyle show were sort of casual. Except for the big production number with Arlington and Andrea, the variety acts would go through their music with the orchestra and then go goof off. The South Pacific number had a large number of dancers who used the entire stage. The stage at the Ernie Pyle Theater was huge, second in size only to the Radio City Music Hall in New York City. It was truly an impressive place to perform. I have photos of the Emanon Trio, (Joe, Dick and I) center stage in this huge theater. We looked like three little cheer leaders on a huge football field.

During the rehearsal period, I was talking to one of the saxophone players in the orchestra and asking him if it was a hard instrument to learn. He said that he had learned pretty easily and started showing me some fingering on the tenor sax.

He had an extra horn in his case and lent it to me to practice on. He showed me the fingering for "Body and Soul" and I started playing at it until the director kicked me out of the rehearsal hall. So I went out into the stairwell and was doing pretty well until a uniformed usher came running up the stairs from the theater. He said that there were some 4,000 people trying to watch a movie and all they could hear is some badly played rendition of Body and Soul. That ended my career on the saxophone.

Although I got along well with Joe Nesbitt, I had a strained relationship with Dick Zappala. We worked well together on stage but off stage, he drove me nuts when, after a performance, he would take off his tux or suit and just throw in on a chair or the floor whichever was closest. I'd get ticked off and pick up after him and hang up his costume so we wouldn't look like a bunch of bums on stage. He was a very talented artist though. His vocal impressions of stars of the movies at that time were well received. He did Jimmy Cagney, Jimmy Stewart, and all usual celebrity impersonations and finished with President Franklin D. Roosevelt, which was a big hit.

Joe Nesbitt was a fantastic pianist who, in civilian life had played for a while with the Lionel Hampton band and had accompanied Sara Vaughn. He had played in his college big band with Mercer Ellington, Duke's son, and was a student of the Schillinger method of notation. Joe's practice sessions consisted of placing little slips of paper, each with a different scale written on it, in a hat and then, reaching in and removing one slip with his left hand and one slip with his right hand. He would then play simultaneously the two scales he had randomly selected.

In addition to playing background music for our

65

act, playing a jazz piano solo and accompanying our musical numbers, Joe's job was to sit quietly at the piano without a word or gesture until at a certain point in the act he would pound the piano keys, jump up and start running around the stage shouting "Three Little Hairs", "Three Little Hairs". I'd grab him and ask him what he thought he was doing running around and shouting right in the middle of our act. I'd say "What's this Three Little Hairs you are shouting about?" Joe would say "Oh, just something I wanted to get off my chest." then he'd go sit down at the piano quietly and never say another word. The audience howled.

Norbert d'Coteau came back stage after our act and said he'd been watching us from the audience and he noted that one lady was laughing so hard she fell out of her seat into the aisle and couldn't get back up. Now, that's funny.

THE HOSPITAL GIGS

After the big show at the Ernie Pyle Theater, we were transferred to a Special Services unit in Yokohama. We were assigned to two CAT gals. These were professional actors who had joined a group called the Civilian Actress Technicians. It was their job to produce shows to travel to Army and Navy bases and hospitals.

A big production was mounted featuring the Emanon Trio, a gal singer named Jackie Edwards and a small combo behind Joe at the piano. We rehearsed the show in which we did our regular act but, incorporated singer Jackie Edwards into a big tap dance finale, which went over very well.

We went on the road in a big bus and toured venues like Yokusuka Naval Hospital, where casualties were flown in directly from the battlefields of Korea. Soldiers who had been wounded that same day were brought in on litters and we got a chance to talk to them while they awaited treatment. They were given the best of medical care within hours of being hit by shrapnel or bullets.

Several memories stick out when I recall those days. We were going from ward to ward entertaining the troops. A couple of orderlies were assigned to push our piano to each ward we visited. We were really happy with the reception we received from the wounded GI's. We got big laughs and lots of applause. The guys were really pleased to be visited by our troop.

Things changed drastically when we entered another ward with about thirty recovering soldiers. Nothing we did seemed to brighten their spirits. The jokes fell flat, the vocals were met with stony stares and the "flash" ending on my tap routine, which usually brought big applause, flopped badly. After the show, we left dejectedly, until informed by the attending nurse, that these patients were Turkish soldiers who understood not a word of English. The "Terrible Turks" were fearless fighters on our side.

The final ward we visited on that one day, brought the horrors of war home to us. Known as the Mental Ward or "Psycho" Ward to some of the inmates, we performed for about twelve patients who acted quite normal and quietly enjoyed our attempts to entertain them While at the same time we were trying to tell jokes and perform musical numbers, we could hear the screams of a patient who was in a padded room being helped by two attendants. It seems the boy was the only surviving member of his company that had been wiped out in a major fire-fight. He was reliving, over and over again, the horror of the action that he had survived.

Several years later, after I was back home in civilian life again, I received a phone call from Dick Zappala, my old Emanon Trio partner. Dick was doing a DJ radio show out of New Jersey, using his vocal impressions to introduce the records he played. He had spoken once to Joe Nesbitt who was back in New York playing with jazz groups.

I never had contact with either of them again. But recently, in trying to find out what became of them, I contacted the musicians union in New York and was told that Joe Nesbitt had died a year or so before.

As for Dick Zappala, I was never able to trace his whereabouts, or whether or not he had survived the years.

SAVING FACE

My first tour of duty with the U.S. Army, was at the end of WWII and a few years prior to the Korean War. I was assigned to General Headquarters and quartered at the old Finance Building in Tokyo, Japan.

Though just a Private First Class, (PFC), I held the rank of Acting Sergeant in my job as military manager of the Service Club, "Ni Ju Ichiban", or in English, Club 21.

Though in the U.S. Army, I was under the command of a civilian, who was the manager of the club.. Elizabeth Mackey was the boss of the several civilian and military personnel who staffed the three story club which catered to Army, Navy, Marines and Air Force enlisted men. Officers had their own clubs, but the enlisted men's facility was top quality. Club 21 offered entertainment, dances and music rooms for sitting and just enjoying the latest recordings. The service club also featured a barber shop, clothes cleaners, shoe shine shops, a restaurant and other services.

While on duty, I filled in as master of ceremonies, stand-up comic, tap dancer and teacher of tap dance classes. It was during a demonstration by a group from the Kodokan Judo Institute, that I was called to save face for my country and my fellow service men. As Master of Ceremonies, I introduced the judo experts from the world famous judo school. Several Japanese teachers and demonstrators took turns tossing each other around on the floor mats. We were impressed by their expertise, especially that of a very slight teen aged girl, who used leverage to throw fighters twice her size.

After the demonstration, the sensei, or head teacher, invited any of our service men to come forward and join in the fun. It was embarrassing when none of our soldiers or sailors would step forward to take part in the show. Especially when the Sensei shamed us by asking why our big, brave American men were afraid of a little Japanese girl. That did it for me. As I have often done when my heart takes over the good common sense of my mind, I accepted the challenge and stepped out onto the floor.

I was asked to take off my shoes and provided with a coarse cotton jacket called an uwabi. It hangs below the buttocks and is tied with a belt called an obi. The sleeves are about three-quarter length. The obi can be of several colors. The finest judo performers can earn the prized "Black Belt". I, of course, was given a basic white belt, as a novice.

I was surprised to note that before I was even matched with an opponent, I was taught the proper way to fall and roll, a technique that, in later days, proved to save me from injury when I took an occasional spill.

After the preliminary instruction, I was matched with a teacher who showed me how to hold my opponent by the coat sleeves and lapels and keep my balance, while moving my feet before trying the "throw". By using their techniques, I was able to use leverage and toss my teacher over my shoulder and to the mat. However, I have a sense that he was being kind and assisted me in my efforts.

The whole episode, which started out as an attempt to "save face" for my fellow G.I.s, became a course of study in the art of Judo which I enjoyed greatly. After returning home from the service, I impressed my heavier pals by putting them on their backs in the gym. I was a different person than the one they use to wrestle to the ground with ease.

BRAINS OVER
BRAWN

While I was still assigned to Club 21 in Tokyo, I had several interesting experiences which called upon quick thinking as a life saving device. One evening, when I was in the middle of MCing a variety show, one of our hostesses came into the room and drew me aside. There was a problem with a drunken sailor down in the lobby, who was threatening to beat up on the little Japanese employees and to throw the hostess down a flight of stairs as well. As an aside, I will note that at the time, I was quite slight of build with a 28 inch waist and weighed about 130 pounds. I was supposed to subdue a 180 pound drunken sailor who was on a rampage.

I guess, as the so-called 'duty officer', it was my responsibility to defuse the volatile situation. While on duty, I was required to wear an arm band that denoted my official capacity. I gave the matter some quick thought and taking off my arm band, I ran up past the sailor, not stopping as I went by him toward the rear entrance. I called back over my shoulder at him, "C'mon buddy!!! Let's get the hell out of here!!! The Shore Patrol is just pulling up in front." I turned again and ran towards the back entrance. The sailor, hearing the urgency in my voice, got on board and not only followed me, but passed me getting out of the building and taking off down the alley.

Heaving the proverbial sigh of relief, I went back inside to congratulate myself for not getting killed or worse. The Shore Patrol did come in right afterwards. I told them I had convinced the sailor to leave on his own accord. They were happy, first of all, that I had saved one of their own from arrest, and secondly, I had saved them from a confrontation with another drunk who was ready to do battle.

ME AND THE GENERAL

The lady in charge of Club 21 in Tokyo, Elizabeth Mackey, was an attractive, mature member of the U.S. Army Hostess Service. The hostesses were civilians, but wore sky blue uniforms and worked as helpers to servicemen in far off areas of the world. Their jobs were to help GIs in need of information or directions. They also acted as dance partners for service men at social functions at the service club.

The ladies I worked with were all very attractive and personable and looked smashing in their blue uniforms. Most of them were single, but had lots of suitors, mostly officers. Their boss, Elizabeth Mackey was a single, middle aged woman who was very pretty, even with the touches of silver in her auburn hair. Miss Mackey had a friend, a handsome man in his sixties, who carried the rank of Brigadier General.

We who served at Club 21, were all invited to a big Christmas party at General Headquarters and I, barely twenty years old and a mere private, was quite surprised when Elizabeth took me by the arm and dragged me over to meet her friend. We were introduced in this quite informal manner. "Pie, I want you to meet Ray. Ray, this is Pie." That is how I met General Piburn. It was like meeting General MacArthur, or some other god. Privates just don't get to rub elbows with generals. Needless to say, as a twenty year old I was very impressed and though usually not at a loss for words, I was tongue-tied. Not having known the protocol for meeting generals, I'm afraid I didn't know whether to salute, shake hands or bow. I probably did all three.

THE BUGLE BOY

I still recall that fateful day
The battle of Bull Run
Our bugle boy, a lad of twelve,
Too small to tote a gun.

He woke us up at 5 a.m.
Still way too dark to see
He roused us from our dreams of home
A playin' reveille.

There warn't a man in all that camp
Awakened by that horn
Who didn't curse that bugle boy,
And the day that he was born.

We broke our camp at sunrise
And started on the march
Without a sip of water
Our throats begin to parch

Our bellies rumbled loud for food
A biscuit and some beans,
Or just a cup of coffee
Was well within their means.

Once again the anger grew
As we trudged without a halt.
When would that bugler sound "Mess Call"?
Our plight seemed all his fault.

Then after what seemed hours
To a halt our column drew
"About time kid", someone yelled
As our little bugler blew.

We'd just been fed and watered
And loafing thereabout
When the bugler called "Assembly"
And the order came, "Move Out!"

We marched ahead a'knowin' soon
The battle would begin.
Just o'er the rise the enemy
Was poised to do us in.

We topped the hill and saw their troops
Across the valley floor.
Then through the air came cold, clear sounds
I'll recall forever more.

Two bugles, one from either side
Called out the sound to charge.
All hell broke loose as men converged
We gathered round our "Sarge".

That fateful day on Henry Hill
July of sixty-one
When brothers fought each other
The battle of Bull Run.

The bugles drove fire through our blood
And gave wings to our feet
The end of day we knew would find
One army in defeat.

If one must lose, the other side
Must then a victor be.
But bullets, swords and cannon fire
Deal death out equally.

At last the bugle call rang out
"Retreat, retreat, retreat."
We gathered up our dead and maimed
And lay them at our feet.

The mournful sound of "Taps" rang out
As prayers for souls were said.
But no sound came from our sad camp,
Our bugle boy lay dead.

Our bugle boy we cursed and jeered
Had only done his job
His calls kept us an army
And not a pointless mob.

He didn't have a rifle
Or any kind of arm
But brave was he as any man
Who faces certain harm.

Non-combatants; bugle boys
And medics and their kind
Go forward into battle
With nothing on their mind

But just to do as duty calls
For country, troops and friend
Ignoring their own danger
Regardless of the end.

Nine hundred died in just one day
In Manassas at Bull Run
But none more brave than our bugle boy,
Just one more mother's son.

© *2004 Ray Toney*

MYSTERIOSO SPIRITUALIS

There comes a time in a person's life, when things happen that are unexplainable in every day terms. At least, there were things that happened, in the course of my life, at which one could only shake one's head and wonder.

I think the term the scientists use is either "Unexplained Phenomena" or simply E.S.P. Extra Sensory Perception.

I may have come by it naturally, as my mother told of a visit from her deceased stepfather the night before his funeral. He appeared in her bedroom and told her to tell her mother that he was all right and not to grieve. Another time she predicted her brother as well as her husband would die at the same time, when the only one ill enough to die was my stepfather. It was a shock when her vision came true and her brother passed within hours of her husband.

I will relate here, three of the several instances I experienced, where the out of the ordinary occurred.

A SPIRITUAL LIFE SAVER....

The first occasion happened as I was driving along the Coast Highway #1, south of San Francisco. This stretch of road is most dangerous and has been the site of many deadly accidents. Its winding two lanes are perched on the very edge of a steep drop to the ocean's surging tide pools, several hundred feet below.

Driving southward, listening to the radio and tapping my fingers on the steering wheel in time to the music, a sudden voice in my head screamed at me to "Get over! Get over!" Just at that instant, an out of control car came speeding around a hairpin turn, directly head on towards me, in my lane.

I had only an instant to react and cut the wheel to the right where, fortunately, there was a wide space for off road parking. I could feel the force of the passing car as it narrowly missed me by inches. As I looked back I could see that the driver of the other car had regained control and resumed his trip in his proper lane.

Angels? Spirit Guides? I can't say. Only that if someone, or something could see around that curve and warn me by shouting clear, concise words into my head and that my brain was in tune to understand and react in time to get out of the way, is some kind of miracle.

A KICK IN THE SEAT OF THE PANTS

This tale takes a little lead up time to consider the state of mind I was in at the time of the event of some distinct note.

A year before, I had just received my Honorable Discharge from the U.S. Army where I had served in the Korean War. During my term of service, I had sustained an injury, which made it difficult to walk without pain. After successful rehab, I was ready to go job seeking. After searching the Help Wanted ads in the newspaper, I was able to set up several interviews, which went very well until I was asked why I hadn't worked for the previous year. As soon as I explained that I had been injured in the service, the attitudes changed and where I was certain I would be hired, I was told that I would be contacted later. Which call I never received.

When I told a friend about my interviews, he told me to never tell a potential employer about my service related injury. He said to tell them my year was spent in travel and enjoying my post army life. He said that the employers didn't want to hire anyone with a possible handicap.

With my newly discovered wisdom, I set up another appointment; this time, with The San Francisco Examiner. The newspaper was advertising for sales reps.

I passed my first interview and was asked to go to another department and take a test. I met a Mr. Habit who had me sit at a table with a test booklet that covered everything from math to English grammar. After the written exam, I was given an oral review. I stumbled badly in this, as I really didn't understand what Mr. Habit was asking of me.

Mr. Habit was perplexed. He said that I had passed the written exam higher than anyone else had in years, yet I was unable to stand up and talk to him face to face. Then I reverted to the old "poor little injured veteran" status and was just about to whine out my story when…. I RECEIVED A REAL, SOLID KICK IN THE PANTS, WHICH I COULD FEEL ON A PHYSICAL LEVEL, AND THE VOICE OF MY LONG DECEASED GRANDFATHER, JOE ATKIN,

YELLED AT ME, "STAND UP AND TALK TO HIM LIKE A MAN!!" Somehow I grew a backbone and I firmly stated. "Mr. Habit, there isn't a job at this paper that I can't do, including yours."

George Habit replied. "That's what I wanted to hear from you. Congratulations. You are a newspaper man."

Was my grandfather watching out for me that day? Did I really hear his voice? Moreover, did I really receive a kick in the buns from Grandpa? All I know, is I got the job thanks to whatever happened that day.

PREVIEW OF COMING ATTRACTIONS

In the movie theater, between shows, the screen will light up with advertising for upcoming films. They show you scenes from the features opening the following week.

A similar showing came to me one evening as I was walking up a hill, battling an oncoming rain and very brisk winds. I was not in a theater but the movie screen in my mind was as bright and clear as any Cinema Scope presentation.

To turn to the "back story", and the reason for my walk in the storm, my wife and I had been talking about moving to Hawaii. I could get a job with a newspaper there. My background as a top producer with the San Francisco Examiner gave me confidence that I could land a job in the land of palm trees and trade winds.

I had been moonlighting as an advertising agent, writing ad copy, doing layouts and writing PR stories for a locally based home building company.

The quality of the company's product, or my advertising genius was making this company grow rapidly to the point where they were building homes in many locations. In point of fact, they were getting to be more than I could handle and still retain my job at the Examiner.

The owner of the homebuilding company lived a couple of blocks away from my home and I phoned him and asked if I could drop over and have a talk with him. I was going to suggest that he find someone else to take over my advertising chores.

I bundled up in warm outerwear and started to walk up the slight grade to the boss's house. With the wind and the rain pelting my face, I bent into the storm and about half way to my destination, I was stopped cold when, like a flash of light that seemed to last only a second, I saw a complete scenario of the actions that were to come just moments later.

In my "Preview of Coming Events", I saw the boss answering his door in a blue silk bathrobe. His little son was alongside him. He invited me in and offered me a cocktail which I declined, I explained the reason for my going over to his house, and heard him say that he had been thinking along the same lines. I heard him make me an offer of a job as his Marketing Manager, handling both the sales force and the ad campaigns. All this I saw and heard before I even reached his house.

The outcome was that everything transpired just as I had seen it in my vision. It was like seeing the same scenes in a movie that you had seen before in the Coming Attractions. It all worked out just as I had seen it in a FLASH. The outcome was that I accepted the job and spent many years in that position. When the company was sold to a large conglomerate, and the owner retired, I accepted an offer from another large homebuilding firm until another employee and I began our own development company.

That was the only time in my life that I had experienced that flash of insight that gave me a quick glimpse into the future. I can't explain it. I don't even try.

ALL MY GOOD AND FAITHFUL FRIENDS.....

My son Brian and his wife, Marie, were suffering through the emotions of losing a pet. Their dog, Maui, a cocker spaniel named after their family's favorite get away vacation spot in the Hawaiian Islands, had died after a long illness.

As I tried to commiserate with Brian, I told him of all the pets that I had as a boy and a newly married man.

I told him that I remembered each of my dog friends. I still know their names and recall their personalities as well as how they looked.

I remember caring for them when they were sick or hurt. And how each of them allowed me to attend their wounds, having trust that I was working on their behalf.

As little Shaggy, a black and white Border Collie mix, lay unconscious in my arms while a neighbor drove us to the veterinary hospital, I recalled telling him "Hold on Shaggy, hold on" while the lump in my ten year old throat grew as I tried not to cry.

We got him there on time and after a stomach pumping cleared the poison from his system, were able to take him home. Shaggy had found some poisoned meat someone in the neighborhood had put out. Two previous dogs I had earlier, had been the victims of a dog poisoner and had died.

Pierre was the first dog we had in our new family after marriage. A white standard poodle breed, he was one of a litter of thirteen pups his mother, Sa Sa, had given birth to. Because he was the runt of the litter, I think we loved him all the more.

Pierre was a dance studio dog. He would accompany my wife Barbara to her dance studio and while the students went through their routines, Pierre would lay quietly down, just inches from their tapping feet and never move a muscle.

One such day, that lasted into evening, I met Barbara at the studio and we went to a little restaurant nearby for a late dinner. When we went inside to eat, she left Pierre in the car. Barbara had just bought a beautiful Ford V8 hard top convertible. It was tomato red with a cream colored top, a red and white "Continental Kit" tire mounted on the rear bumper, and gorgeous cream and red leather upholstery. When we left the restaurant to go home, Barbara was shocked to find her beautiful leather upholstery in shreds. Pierre was teaching us a lesson... "Don't dare leave me alone".

The car I drove was a new Studebaker two door sports car that had the reputation of looking like it was going forward and backward at the same time. Its front hood tapered down from the windshield to the front bumper and its rear trunk was also sloped down to the rear bumper at about the same degree of slant. I kept noticing a lot of scratches on the rear trunk surface leading from the back window down to the rear bumper. We couldn't figure out what was causing the scratches. One day, we made a big production of going out. I put Pierre into the garage from the kitchen. We left the house, got into Barbara's car, started the motor, yelled "Good Bye" to Pierre and drove off down the street, A few doors down, we stopped the car and snuck back into the house. Tiptoeing into the kitchen we opened the kitchen door to the garage a crack in time to spot Pierre climbing up onto the roof of the low slung car, and sliding down the rear deck like a kid in a playground. He was shocked we caught him but how can you get angry at such ingenuity?

Pierre was with us from our first house where we lived before Brian was born. When we first moved into the Briarwood home in Santa Clara, we hadn't done any rear yard landscaping and the winter rains brought mud. Some dog owners think they are the only kooks concerning their pups but we were just as bad. Before Pierre, (nickname "PeePee Pierre") went out to do his business, we had to put four rubber doggie galoshes on him (one for each of his little feet.) It was funny to watch him try to walk in his strap-on rubber boots. He would lift each foot, way up in the air, before stepping forward.

While we were building our new home in Saratoga, Pierre shared our little two bedroom rental apartment which had the disadvantage of having to walk him for his daily duties. Fortunately our land lady was an absentee owner and we had to sneak him in and out so she wouldn't catch on that we had a pet.

When the new house was completed, we moved to Saratoga, California.

Pierre had a favorite resting spot under a china cabinet in the family room. One day, a year or so later, I could see he was not feeling well and I couldn't get him to come out from under the cabinet. He finally came out on unsteady legs. He lost control of his bowels and was so embarrassed. I called the vet who said to bring him right in. I took him out to the car but his strength was so dissipated I had to lift him to get him into the front seat and drove him to the Vet. I left him there for overnight watching. The next morning we got a call that he was not doing well and wasn't expected to live. It seems that when Pierre had got out of the yard and wandered away, he had probably rubbed up against some bushes with poisonous spray on it.

The vet felt that he was not purposefully poisoned or he would have died much more quickly. I wanted to go right over but the Vet said it was not a good idea as it would upset him too much. So we never got to be there when he died. As the first dog of our new family, we were extremely upset. But time has a way of eliminating the sadness and leaving only the glad memories. And so it is.

There are a thousand more memories that pop up when one thinks of their old pets, which have gone before. One thought is of Chow who was a mixed Chow/terrier pup whose big chow dog head was so big, that his hind legs would come up off the floor when he dug his head into his bowl to eat. And how Shaggy would pick a fight with a bigger dog, and then run and stand between the front legs of Pal, our big German Shepherd and bark at the bigger dog and dare him to take on his big brother.

Shaggy got into a lot of trouble. Mom cooked a roast beef every Sunday for dinner. After dinner we all went into the living room to sit around the radio and listen to the Jack Benny show. Mom had left the clean up until after the radio show with all the dishes still on the table. We were shocked to see Shaggy running out of the kitchen with the left over half of our roast beef in his mouth.

After Pierre, we wanted another white standard poodle to take his place. At that time standards were hard to find. Especially white ones, so one day we found a breeder in Stockton, Clalifornia, who advertised silver standards, We drove up and looked at the litter and picked a black pup who we were assured by the breeder would turn silver as he got out of the puppy stage. Now we all know that Jacques never did turn silver except for a few white hairs as he aged.

Jacques drove me nuts from the time we brought him home. He was so lonely the first few nights that he howled and yipped all night long. Alarm clocks and one of our T-shirts didn't do the trick. He was also very headstrong and wouldn't learn to obey. Finally, Barbara took him to obedience school so he would come when called and not run out into the street and get hit by a car.

I have terrific memories of Jacques and his very haughty personality. I would laugh when, after he broke loose with a stinky, I would hold my nose and say "Whew...Jacques." He would get an indignant look on his face that was priceless. Barbara would admonish me "Don't laugh at him, you hurt his feelings."

87

Jacques could be sound asleep in another room but if Barbara just lightly opened the lid on the cookie jar, he would be in the kitchen in a flash. There were two brands of crackers that we purchased. One was Ritz the other Hi Ho. Jacques was very particular about his selection. If we offered him a Hi Ho cracker he would dance around and beg for one. If he was offered a Ritz Cracker, he would yawn and walk away. Personally I can't tell the difference between the two crackers but if it wasn't a Hi Ho, Jacques seemed to say, "Forget you".

We all have our individual memories of Jacques but my one outstanding one is of holding him in my arms to calm him while the Vet administered the last goodbye.

I had fought it, though the rest of the family noted that it was the humane thing to do. But after seeing that the medications could not give him back his ability to stand or control his bodily functions, I gave in and Brian and I drove him to his last Vet appointment. I left Brian outside to wait for me while Jacques closed his eyes and went to his final rest.

Afterward, I walked away to be alone. I motioned for Brian to give me a little space to get it together, while that same lump in the throat I had experienced while taking little Shaggy to the vet, receded to a point where I could talk without breaking.

The sad parts have all slipped away and the good memories, which far outstripped the bad, remain.

And so it is.

CO-INCIDENCE... OR...??

The following is one of the strangest cases of co-incidence that I have ever experienced. Or, was it co-incidence? If not, I do not the purpose of the happening and as far as I know, no great occurrence of any kind as a result.

In 1950, during the action know as the "Korean Conflict", I was stationed in Tokyo, Japan. My duty, as a Special Service Specialist in the U.S. Army, was as a manager of a service club know as "Club Niju Ichiban". Translated into English, "Club 21".

Many service men and women who came to Tokyo during those years, may recall the splendid facility that was Club 21. It offered off duty service people a place to relax, have fun and be entertained.

Club 21 was an imposing two story building that housed a huge ballroom, a stage for bands and entertainers, writing rooms, a restaurant and a billiard parlor. The full basement had a barber shop, shoe shine stand, a cleaning and pressing facility and many other necessary services.

The billiard room was quite large, featuring eight pool tables, two billiard tables and a snooker table. The manager of the facility was a Japanese of quite some international fame. Kinrey Matsuyama was a former World's Billiard Champion, having beaten the master of the billiard cue, Willie Hoppe, in a 1929 tournament.

"Matsy" Matsuyama, as Time Magazine described him was "just two inches taller than his 57" billiard cue and casts a giant shadow upon the green baize background of billiards." (Feb. 18, 1929). He could barely reach over the table he so masterfully commanded. He had snow white hair which he combed straight back. His ready sense of humor was accompanied by a grin that turned up on one side of his mouth. He was immediately likeable at my first meeting with him.

I developed a friendship with "Matsy" and for the sixteen months I worked at the club, I would supply him with his favorite brand of American pipe tobacco which he kept burning in his ever present briar. In return, I received lessons in handling a cue stick from a World Champion. It was like getting boxing lessons from Mohammed Ali or chess lessons from Bobby Fisher.

When my tour of duty was over, I said goodbye to my friend and as I left, the "Chanp" presented me with a gift of a hand made pool cue. Knowing that my home was in San Francisco, Matsuyama asked me to deliver another cue stick to a friend of his who owned a widely known billiard parlor on Market Street. Welker Cochrane was also a former World Champion and his establishment was the gathering place for the greatest devotees of the sport in the San Francisco Bay Area.

I met Mr. Cochrane and passed "Matsy"'s gift on to him. When everyone there heard that I had come from Matsuyama, they all crowded around wanting to know about him and his protégé, Miss Katsura.

Katsura San was one of the few women billiard players who was developing a world wide reputation. I later had the opportunity to see Katsura play on American television. She was one of the first women players to be televised in the United States.

My first job on being separated from the service, was with the San Francisco Examiner, the newspaper known as the Monarch of the Dailies.

After I had been with the Examiner for a year or so, I was walking up Market Street on my way to the office. It was about mid day and I was surprised to come face to face with a short gentleman with white hair. Both shock and recognition hit as we looked at each other. Kinrey Matsuyama, my friend from Tokyo, Japan, had come to the U.S.A. to visit Welker Cochrane and we were both surprised to meet on a crowded street in a city of 600,000 people.

We greeted each other warmly but, unfortunately I had to get back to the paper to meet a deadline and we had to say goodbye. We were still in awe of the coincidental meeting in a city 3,000 miles from Tokyo, to which he soon returned.

Co-incidence? More than likely, however, that is not the end of the story.

Another year or so went by. Still employed by the same newspaper, I was walking down Market Street and happened to walk into a large department store. I was moving through the aisles when I heard a voice say, "Toney San!" the Japanese equivalent of Mr. Toney! I turned around and was once again, surprised to see Kinrey Matsuyama.

He had returned to San Francisco and was shopping in the same store I happened to enter.

The wonder of time, space and what? Effect? The wonder of two people to be in the same location at the same time in a greater area of over one million people is not totally out of the question, but to have the same two people repeat the meeting after being three thousand miles and two years between times, that makes one wonder. Doesn't it?

If either Matsuyama or I had started our walks a few seconds earlier or later, if I had not interrupted my journey to go into a store at the same time "Matsy" was there, or taken another aisle on opposite sides of the store….if….if….if. It is still a wonder to me.

As the King of Siam said to Anna,
"Is a Puzzlement."

BABY TEETH

A Touch Of Nonsensical Whimsy

Oh, where do our baby teeth go?
A myst'ry that we ought to know.

Consider it sound
That at sixty per pound
And considering it just as before
In just four thousand years
Or eons my dears
Somewhere there must be
Quite a mound.

Now the average child,
Intemperate, or mild,
Has a total of twenty and eight
And before he is ten,
Exudes them and then,
Has thirty-two more to create.

In China alone,
It is certainly known
That the yellow race
Breeds quite a lot.
And in each Chinese child
There are teeth that grow wild
Then drop out of the mouths
Of each tot.

And in France you can bet
From Marie Antoinette
To de Gaule and that pipsqueek Gigot
Each babe had his share

Of molars and hair
But just where did those
Little teeth go?

Oh, where do our baby teeth go?
A myst'ry that we ought to know.

You can bet without fear
Of losing, my dear,
That each one of us has had a full head.
But over the years,
We've had but two ears
And both have stayed put
Until we're dead.

Now permanent teeth
Can be found on the heath
In the meadow or any old field
They are used in old rings,
In necklaces on strings
So we know to great age they won't yield.

It's established as fact
That no one has lacked
His quota of primary ivory
And there isn't a doubt,
That when they're cast out
Through some well executed connivery ,

There must be some plan
By God or by man
For disposal of tons of this crockery.
But where is the key
To this strange mystery
That has made all our efforts
A mockery?

Oh, where do our baby teeth go?
A myst'ry that we ought to know.

Anthropologist chaps,
With crudely made maps,
Have discovered the bones of our forebears
And in each grinning skull
There are molars to cull,
To prove ages old teeth still are more there.

And in each moldy grave,
There are second sets saved
To further thicken the plots
And the mummies of old
Have adult teeth I'm told,
But where are the teeth of the tots?

So answer me please if you will
Where is that ivory hill?

The graveyard of the elephants
Is hidden well away,
The baby teeth of the saber tooth
Cannot be found today,
But neither can the baby teeth
Of our darling Doris Day.

Oh, where do our baby teeth go?

THE CURSE OF
THE BOTTLE IMP

One of the classic mystery tales of the nineteenth century was penned by arguably, the most popular author of his day, Robert Lewis Stevenson. Written in 1893, the story was dramatized as a radio production, in which I was cast, in 1948 .

The story follows a bottle of spirits, rum I think, and its consecutive owners throughout many years. The bottle comes with a curse attached which, will bring its owner untold wealth and good fortune. The catch is this: if the owner of the bottle dies with it in his possession, his soul goes immediately to hell. So the trick is to find someone who will buy it from you before you die. The curse and its down side, must be divulged to any prospective buyer. Another catch is that the bottle can only be sold for less than it was purchased.

The bottle goes from owner to owner, each of whom, becomes fabulously rich while owning it, all the while knowing he must divest himself of owner-ship before he dies and loses his soul to Satan. One of the last owners has a major problem. He purchased the bottle for one cent, American. His fortune becomes vast but he tries to figure out how to sell the bottle for less than he paid. He gets the bright idea of traveling to France where the lowest denomination of currency is the "centime" which at the time was of lesser value than a U.S. Cent.

The show was called "The Veteran's Theater Of The Air" and was broadcast live on Sunday afternoons. Of several voices I played, my final character was an old seaman, who purchased the bottle, knowing he could not sell it for any less, but as his speech went, "I could care less, I'm going to Hell anyway.", or words to that effect, and he uncorks the bottle and drains its contents.

On radio shows, there was no need to learn all the lines as on stage or television. You read through the script a few times and then performed it, page by page. To avoid the sound of rustling paper as one turned pages, the radio scripts were single sheets, not stapled. As you finished reading the speech on one sheet you quietly removed it from the top and slipped it under the rest of the script. Here is where my part of the curse came into being. As I was reading the speech of the Old Sea Dog, when I got to the bottom of the page, I carefully removed the top sheet to slide it to the bottom of the stack. Static electricity or vacuum or some such phenomenon, attached the next sheet of the script to the one I was removing and out of the corner of my eye, I saw the continuation of my speech floating quietly to the floor.

There were three of us actors grouped around a single boom mike placed at about the level of our mouths. I could not, in the middle of the speech, break it off and reach down to the floor to retrieve the lost sheet of paper with the rest of the seaman's dialogue, so, in character, I started ad libbing the speech. I had always been taught that whether acting or in a dance routine, never stop. Don't let the audience know you've "gone up". I recall that I even started singing, "Sixteen Men On A Dead Man's Chest, Yo Ho Ho and a Bottle of Rum!" No doubt shaking up the director, my fellow actors and probably, causing a disturbance in the tomb of RLS.

Finally, one of the actors sharing my microphone, saw the problem and stuck his script in front of me where I could take up where I was supposed to be in the story.

If you, by chance, were tuned in to Veterans' Theater of The Air for that broadcast of Robert Lewis Stevenson's The Bottle Imp, I am sure you never knew there was a break in the action. Because it was radio and not television you couldn't see the look of abject terror on my face, or the quizzical consternation of the faces of the other actors on that particular boom mike.

I guess that is one of the things that endeared me to live performances. No one knows when the "IMP" will strike and a curse will go into effect. There have been many other times over the years that I have seen actors get completely lost when memorized lines fail to come forth. When you see that look, you know you are in trouble and it is time to start ad libbing* again.

* ad lib. Going off script and making up dialogue as one goes along.

THE VISITOR

It was only by chance that I happened to look out my bedroom window towards the open land behind my home. Even then, if I hadn't seen just an infinitesimal movement, I would not have noticed the figure standing quite still under an oak tree.

I watched for several minutes, wondering what had drawn this entity to my house in the hills. From the distance of perhaps forty feet, I could make out the features, especially the dark, flinty eyes that held no expression.

The uncanny thing was the unmoving stillness that seemed to be a means of blending into the background, unseen, watching. But there! There again was the slight movement of the head. More like an unintended paroxysm or a spasm for a split second and then, back to the unflinching, staring stillness.

I wondered, as I surreptitiously surveyed my visitor, if my surveillance was somehow perceived by the subject of my observance.

I took note of the physical particulars of this being and was impressed by the ramrod straight back, the slightly tilted head set upon a neck that seemed almost too long to support it and finally, its almost military bearing. I estimated the height to be anywhere between four and five feet as it stood. Taller than a small child but shorter than an average adult.

Knowing that my story would not be believed in its telling, I rushed to get my digital camera to have a visual affirmation of my visitor's appearance. It was as though the presence of a camera raised a warning flag and as I snapped the first picture, the stillness evaporated from the being and moving off to my right, it walked purposefully and steadily out of my line of sight, behind a small mound of earth.

I dashed to the other end of the house, looking to see if I could get another picture from a different angle. The only full view I had was from the window over my kitchen sink and I took another picture. At this time I truly felt that my presence was indeed being felt for it made a one hundred eighty degree turn and slowly, deliberately, walked back to the place where I had originally made the observation. Except the new position was definitely behind a tree, where I could not get a clear view.

As this observation had now exceeded fifteen minutes or so, I felt it time to force the issue and make myself known to my uninvited guest. I slowly opened my rear door and, holding my camera at the ready, I eased out onto the back walk but as I aimed the lens, two exceptionally long wings unfolded and with a downward thrust elevated the graceful blue heron into its normal element. I watched as it circled away from me and went on its way.

I can't imagine what brought this beautiful giant of a bird to my rear yard. I have no water for it to bathe and wade in. No aquatic flora or fish upon which to feed. I just assume that it chose to visit a fellow being who would marvel at its beauty and natural grace. And I am grateful that it selected me to be awed by one of nature's finest creations.

October 3, 2006 ~ Ray Toney
Coarsegold, California

ALLERGIES

Of this land's geography,
I have roamed from sea to sea
In search of such a place,
I've yet to find.

For in every dale and town,
There is not a piece of ground
That gives me peaceful rest
And peace of mind.

It seems wherever I may roam,
Each place that I'd consider home,
Has dander, mites and pollen
In the air.

All the dogs and cats and trees,
Inflame my sensitivities
With tiny bits of ragweed,
Dust and hair.

So tell me, where upon this earth.
All around its mighty girth,
Is such a place where I
Can get relief.

If you know, then tell me please,
Where I'll not have to sneeze or wheeze
And free me from this
Allergenic grief.

REUNION

We met for such a short time
Yet, in that hour or so,
The years apart floated away
As if they had not been.

Once again the joy of the moment
Washed over me. I delighted
In her very presence. I had worried
That ten years might have changed
Us both enough that I might have
Not recognized her. As she entered
The restaurant, I saw the same wavy
Blonde hair, the blue, blue, eyes and
Knew that the years hadn't dimmed
My memories.

I arose from the table and strode
Purposefully to greet her. As her
Searching gaze locked onto me,
I could see first, recognition and then
Delight as her smile glowed across the
Space of the dining room.
Her fingers lightly fluttered over her
Heart as she took a little catch breath.

As we talked and brought each other
Up to date on our lives those past
Years, I relived the many good
And delightful times together,
Although knowing these were

Just gossamer threads upon which
Memories are woven, ethereal
Clouds whose substance dissipates
As dreams vanish with awakening.

And then, all too soon, the real world
Beckons. Real time, suspended for such
A short interval, starts its march
Forward toward the horizon unknown.

We embraced for one last time
And as she turned and walked
Away I felt a part of my life ebbing
From me and once again I knew sorrow.

ASPIRING TO MEDIOCRITY

As generations pass we are noticing a falling away of quality in all phases of life. The arts; music, acting, play writing, painting.

It is not that the talent to produce quality is not there, it is only that those who aspire to becoming artists are not well versed in what excellence is. Having grown up with a certain declining quality of talent over the years, generation after generation sees only the worst and therefore sees it as a standard by which to aim for.

Young actors are cast right out of school, not because of talent but because they have the "right look" for a character in a television play. Most cannot deliver a line distinctly or with feeling. The demands of the monster, television, do not allow time for a character to "get into" a role, as a stage actor is able to do.

In "Singing In The Rain" one of the most appreciated MGM musical comedy motion pictures of a few years back, actors Don Lockwood (Gene Kelley) and Cosmo Brown, (Donald O'Connor) are assigned to a diction coach who is supposed to teach them to enunciate properly so that they can be understood in delivering dialogue. Though the scene and the situation is farcical, the idea of teaching actors to deliver a line distinctly seems to have been lost in the shuffle of pounding out weekly television series episodes.

I have trouble understanding what most young actors are saying. But even in silent picture days, the idea of the story seemed to get over, so who cares if the dialogue is indistinguishable from talking with a mouth full of Quaker's oatmeal.

I thought that as I advanced in years, my hearing was not as good as it should be. Then, after changing channels and finding an old black and white movie with real actors in the roles, I noticed that I distinctly heard each syllable spoken.

Most of the old actors in motion pictures and television had a background of working on stage to live audiences. They learned their craft or, they were out of work. They also learned timing. The most important part of acting, other than delivering a line distinctly and with feeling, is knowing when to speak and when to "hold it for the laugh". Which brings me to the topic of comedy.

One of the most over used technical aspects of television production is the "laugh track". Truly funny material, which was performed before a live audience as "All In The Family" or "Three's Company" drew laughs because the writing and the timing of the delivery, was truly funny.

Because audiences grew up with the majority of the television shows they watched of poor quality, they began to accept mediocrity, (and worse), as the norm. They did not know enough to demand quality writing and acting in television.

The medium has been called "the electronic baby sitter". It allows children of all ages, (even into their forties and fifties), to be hypnotized into sitting in front of an electronic device that provides, action and color, BUT lacks the requirement to need to think about what is going on. The laugh track tells them when to laugh and what is funny. They do not have to make up their own minds about what is entertaining and what is not.

The music industry is just as much at fault, in that composers and recording artists pander to the lowest possible denominator of music consumers. That which is provided today is mostly not musical. Rapper MC Hammer said he started rapping because he couldn't sing.

Composers like Mozart and Bizet were so knowledgeable in their craft that they wrote symphonic masterpieces when in their teens. Bizet was only seventeen in 1855, when he composed his Symphony in C Major, a work, which was hailed as extraordinary, when dusted off and restaged in 1934.

What sells today are not clever, romantic lyrics but boringly repetitive, demeaning words of a violent nature. Compare the majority of today's writers of popular music to the lyrics of Lorenz Hart, Oscar Hammerstein II or Cole Porter. Their lyrics were clever, romantic and deliciously descriptive in content.

Perhaps the pendulum will swing back to where intelligence will once again override the commonplace and force writers, directors and performers to improve upon their presentations. Unless the public demands better quality, they will get only what they are being fed. Which is not an acceptable norm.

THE LEFT HANDED SIX-GUN

Long before he starred on Highway to Heaven and Little House On The Prairie, Michael Landon became a major television star as Little Joe Cartwright, on "Bonanza".

Upon meeting him the first time, I was quick to realize that "Little Joe" wasn't little at all. He appeared to me to be well over six feet tall and had a lean, athletic build.

I picked him up at the San Francisco Airport on a Friday evening. Dressed in his western gear, complete with boots and cowboy hat, he had gone directly from the studio, to the airport in LA, to catch the flight to the Bay Area.

Michael Landon had come to make a guest appearance at the Grand Opening of a community of new and expensive homes in the San Jose area. As the representative of the building company, Duc & Elliot Builders, I was nominated to set up a schedule of radio interviews to advertise the Sunday event. On Saturday afternoon, I picked Michael up at his hotel in Los Altos and drove to the radio station, KEEN in San Jose for the first interview.

Radio KEEN broadcast from their studios on an upper floor, in the De Anza Hotel. I parked the car and we went up to the studio where the interview went very well. As we left KEEN and headed back to the car, I turned around and there was no Michael Landon behind me. I went back to the lobby of the

De Anza and there was "Little Joe" surrounded by a group of youngsters, chatting and signing autographs.

On the way to our next appointment, Michael noted that he hadn't had time to pack a pair of swim trunks and asked if I could stop at a men's store, in downtown, San Jose. He wasn't in the store more than three or four minutes at most, but between the time he left the store and walked half way across the sidewalk to my car, he was mobbed again by a group of children who recognized him, even out of costume.

Where those two sets of kids came from, I'll never know, but it was as if they had a group sixth sense that led them to that spot where Michael Landon would be, if only for a moment. As columnist Leigh Weimers of the San Jose Mercury and News put it "Call it star quality."

On Sunday, the day of the big opening celebration, Michael dressed in his Bonanza costume again and wore his Colt revolver, in its left-handed holster. He graciously autographed hundreds of 8x10 glossy photographs for the big line of kids who showed up to see "Little Joe Cartwright".

After the appearance at Oak Dell Ranch, he picked up his gear at his hotel and we went to the San Francisco International airport where he caught his flight back to Los Angeles.

On Monday morning, as I was getting out of the car at my office, I looked into the back seat and found that, in his hurry to get packed and to the airport, Michael had left his holstered Colt revolver behind.

I can't tell you that I didn't think about purloining that particular piece of paraphernalia. The temptation was there, but my conscience, would have bothered me forever. So I packaged the pretty pistol and posted it first class to his palatial residence in Pasadena.

(No, he didn't live in Pasadena but the temptation to add another "P" word was too great.)

Leigh Weimers

Writing's on wall for supervisors: Redistrict or else

Landon

BACKWARD GLANCES — The death of Michael Landon reminded San Josean Ray Toney of what he calls the actor's automatic ability to draw attention without trying. It was in the early '60s, at the height of popularity of the "Bonanza" TV show, and Toney had engaged Landon to appear at the opening of a Cupertino subdivision. They'd taped an interview at the old KEEN studios in the De Anza Hotel, and Toney was heading for their next stop when he noticed Landon wasn't with him. "I went back into the lobby," he says, "and there was 'Little Joe,' surrounded by a group of youngsters, chatting away and signing autographs." It happened again when Landon asked to stop at a downtown men's store. "He wasn't in the store more than three or four minutes at most," notes Toney, "but between the time he left the store and walked halfway across the sidewalk toward my car, he was mobbed again by a group of children who recognized him, even out of costume. Where those two sets of kids came from I'll never know, but it was as though they had a group sixth sense that led them to that spot where Michael Landon would be, if only for a moment." Call it star quality... **John**

A DISSERTATION ON THE POSSIBILITIES OF THE MELDING OF SPIRITUAL AND PHYSICAL BODIES IN MAN

There have been many writings both ancient and modern that speak of the two bodies of man, The Spiritual and the Physical.

In the New Testament, St. Paul taught about the duality of the makeup of man in his letter to the Corinthians (I Cor. 15:44) "There is a natural body and a spiritual body."

More recently, in the eighteenth century, American statesman Benjamin Franklin stated, "We are spirits! That bodies should be lent us in order that we may acquire knowledge, experience pleasure and aid us in assisting our fellow creatures, is a kind and benevolent act of God."

The spiritual body has boundless energy and limitless capabilities. When melded into a physical being, spirit is confined in the limited space of a human embryo, unable to soar and move at will. As the embryo grows, the spiritual body is able to extend its reach and teaches the physical how to respond to thought.

Those spirits, who have already grown and learned their lessons in living on the physical plane, are able to pass on their acquired knowledge to the developing beings. All of this knowledge originates on the higher levels of spiritual existence. Mathematics, musical ability, (which in itself is a combination of mathematics and art), the healing arts, architecture and the multitudes of necessary sciences and disciplines needed to improve life on the physical plane must be inculcated into the growing minds of newly formed beings.

Each new entity must gain knowledge of many needed subjects, just to exist in the physical world. Some are inclined to particular fields and become masters of those arts. They become teachers to others who have the desires to acquire those abilities and become proficient in them.

As spirit and physical body become more attuned, spirit's desire to experience its natural, unfettered freedom to move through space may be epitomized by the young, lithe Olympians who continue to surpass each other by actually flying through the air as they perform astounding feats of acrobatics. What used to be amazing tumbling moves, incorporating 'hand springs', 'round offs', 'flip flops' and culminating with a full back flip in the air, have been surpassed by a final move of a full double rotation back flip without touching the ground. This is not the action of a mass of muscle and bone but the work of spiritual mind controlling the physical.

Spirit must learn that it must not require of its physical counterpart, more than it is capable of doing. Though spirit is indestructible, its physical home is subject to being damaged and even destroyed. Though spirit enjoys the feeling of freedom experienced by speeding down a road at one hundred miles per hour in a motorized vehicle, a sudden stop can finalize its journey on earth.

As it is spirit which is in control, it must conscientiously see to the care and maintenance of its physical dwelling. In other words, a good, healthy body is necessary for spirit to accomplish its work and further development.

To put it another way, assume you, (spirit), are in a car, (your body) and as you are going on your journey, you ignore the warning lights which indicate you are out of oil in the crank case. You keep on driving until the motor burns out and freezes up. This vehicle is no longer able to be your means of transportation. There is no alternative but to step out of it and leave it to rust alongside the road.

Those spirits, who ignore the care of their physical home, may one day be looking down at their body in a box and thinking, "I should have taken better care of it."

FULL CIRCLE

The mother placed a cool cloth on the daughter's forehead and spoke softly to her. You could see the tenderness as her loving hands caressed the feverish brow. The mother's eyes held a glint of moisture that she blinked away so that no one could see the pain she suffered along with that of the daughter.

The father, who had provided for the daughter's every need as she grew to womanhood, turned and left the room, knowing that nothing he could do, no work for his hands or wallet freely opened to her could help now. Besides, men do not cry in the presence of others, if they can help it. A man's tears are a solitary happening, alone in his room or walking rapidly into the wind. A wind to blow away the sorrows only men can experience.

The daughter, attached to the morphine drip that hopefully numbed the pain she had felt when she entered the hospital, appeared comatose. Her unseeing eyes opened only to mere slits. The nurses had said that the hearing is the last of the senses to go and those in attendance were cautioned to be careful of what was said out loud.

One could visualize a time some four decades before when the same mother and father had hovered over their same sick child and ministered the tender care that was given now. Yet, here the three of them were in the same dance of mercy and love, only knowing that this was the last dance and the time was coming for the music to stop forever.

The brother, a big fellow who wielded the tools of his trade with masterful force, held his sister's hand as though it were a delicate bird and spoke lovingly to her, recalling their days together as children growing up. The bond of siblings, stronger than ever at this time. All through the many nights he sat at her bedside, catching a short nap in between cautious watching and waiting.

What circle had brought them all back together in this little hospital room? One of them suffering excruciating physical pain, only alleviated by drugs, the other three suffering pain which no drug could allay.

A SOUL IN ORBIT

A Revelation

The age-old questions considered by thinking, intelligent beings, "Who Am I?", "What Is My Purpose In being On Earth?" and ultimately, "Where Do I Go When I Leave This Earth?", come back time and again to haunt our inquisitive minds.

Consider this; that Who we are might well be the "Tools Of God", the Fingers and Hands of the Great Intelligence, doing the work and implementing the Master Plan of the Master. That the Great Intelligence exists, is beyond a doubt for any individual who takes the time to consider his surroundings and makes an effort to communicate with that Intelligence. But these pages have not been set aside to convince the skeptics, only to allow the thinker some ideas for contemplation.

In addition to the implementation of God's plans for the development of His community, another reason for our being here is to learn to be a part of a higher society to which we will ultimately be adjoined. Such society will not tolerate a mind steeped in negativity, but only the mind, which has learned to eradicate all thoughts of hate and fear, learning to express love as its primary emotion.

As to where we go when we leave here, that plane may be reached when we have not only learned the lessons of loving our fellow creatures, but have striven to pass on, by word and example, that which we have been fortunate enough to have assimilated.

What are the means by which we, as evolving souls, make our way through this journey of life? In other words, how did we get here, from our place of origination? How do we return? As a simile, which we can couch in modern, space age terms, picture a space shuttle mounted on a rocket engine, as it lifts off slowly, then increasing speed until it gains the momentum to force it into orbit around the earth. This orbit can be described as an ellipse, meaning that it leaves its destination at an angle that drives it into an egg-shaped pattern rather oval in design and then returns to its place of origin.

The further out the rocket sends the space craft, the less it is affected by the pull of gravity. However, in its orbital pattern, as the rocket gets closer to earth, the force of gravity pulls it in closer and closer to its point of lift off.

Following that line of thought, substitute "heaven", for want of a word describing the launching pad comparable to that on earth, and the human soul, or spirit, in place of the space shuttle noted above. When launched into its life on earth, the soul begins its journey when the pull of "gravity" of the soul's original birthplace, is the strongest.

However as the young incarnate sees all the wonders around him and begins to move onward, experiencing life and learning how to control its new physical body, it draws further away from its spiritual home.

The youngster lies on his back in a field of green grass and wonders at the beauty of the clouds overhead, the vastness of the mountains and the greatness

116

of the forests. As he grows through the beginnings of his life here on earth, he begins to learn more and more about this new place he has been thrust into. The child notes the bee sucking the nectar from a blossom and plucking the flower from the stem, sips the sweetness from the flower and wonders how and why this delightful sensation can exist in a colorful cluster of petals.

He hurries through childhood and into his teens, then, finally, into his adult years. As he advances, he strives to live, as well as learn. He now tries to use that which he has become competent in, to aid others who have joined him in this journey.

When he reaches his middle years, it can be described as his apogee, or furthest point away from his original beginnings. At this point, the pull from his point of origin becomes stronger. He begins to wonder about his beginnings and contemplates the end of his journey on earth. What will become of him? Will he fade into nothingness? Will all the knowledge he has worked so hard to attain, be wasted in a mind that will cease to exist? Will the journey through this life be worth anything in terms of accomplishment and who will be there to pat him on the back and say, "Job well done, good and faithful servant"?

As he goes into his late maturity, he begins to feel the pull, back to his original starting point, stronger and stronger. He begins to lose interest in the ways of this world and begins to think about going "Home". Yet he worries about whether or not he will be able to get back safely. He doesn't understand how to make his return back to where he began, before his birth on this earth.

But he need not fear. The plan is sure, well conceived and his road lies clearly marked before him. As the pull of the earth's gravity assures the return of the orbiting space craft to its homeland, so does the pull of God's Homeland draw every soul back to the point of its beginning, unerringly and safely.

Your Heavenly Father, who has sent you on this mission, stays well in touch with you. Just as Mission Control guides the shuttle back in safety to its home base, so will God guide you back home when the time is right, according to plan.

ARE YOU LISTENING?
REALLY LISTENING?

Did you ever have someone explain directions to their home to you? And did you get on the road and then not quite remember what you were told? It has happened to me. Many times.

I have tried to get to my destination based on the directions given but when I got a certain distance into my trip...things got a little fuzzy. "Did he say left at the school?" "Was I supposed to go right back at the last intersection?" "Was it Commercial Ave. or Commonwealth Drive"?

We stop and wonder why we didn't get the directions right in the first place. We know the answer. We listened to the directions but didn't really hear them.

Do we really listen when the "small still voice within" gives us direction in our lives? The message is there but so many things interfere with our concentration that somehow, the thought that was there a minute ago...that seemed very important, was shoved aside by outside interference. The weekly, "must see" television show. The car radio, continually pumping out music, advertising and news. The sound of a car horn, out on the street. A dog barking. A telephone ringing.

Is it any wonder that we never get the message that can mean life, death, mishaps, good fortune or a warning of imminent danger?

I recall driving down a winding, two lane road on the Pacific Coast Highway, late one night. It was quite dark and there was very little traffic. I don't think I was quite alert as I should have been. All of a sudden, a not so small and still voice yelled at me in my mind's ear, "MOVE OVER! GET OFF THE ROAD!!!" That warning alerted me and as I was starting to drive around a curve, another car, speeding and out of control came right at me on my side of the road. I was able to pull out of the way and was saved from a terrible accident.

A woman who worked in a major department store in San Jose told me of sitting at her desk in the accounting department, when a voice in her head told her to get up from her chair and move away. She had no sooner obeyed, when a large lighting fixture dropped straight down onto her desk and the chair she had been occupying seconds before.

Does God send us the answers to our prayers only to find out that no one is at home to receive them? It's like placing a classified ad in the newspaper or Craig's List and then not staying at home to receive calls from interested parties.

EL GATO

They came from, I don't know where, mewing out a story that I could not understand, not knowing cat talk.

They spoke very vociferously, trying to express their feelings or needs. They looked up at me, trying to impress me with eye contact.

There were two of them, obviously from the same litter, no longer kittens but far from adulthood. The one, a beautiful orange color and the other a standard, gray striped tabby. Entwining themselves around my legs, they were looking for contact of some kind. As I assumed they were looking for a bit of food, I thought about what I had in the larder that would satisfy a cat's diet. The only thing I could think of was some cold cereal. I had never owned a cat, but knew my neighbors fed theirs some sort of commercial dry cat food.

I went into the house and poured some cereal into a bowl and took it back out to where I had left them. They were gone. Just as quickly as they had come, they had gone and left me with a bowl of dried cereal. I set the bowl down in case they came back. The cereal was untouched for a day or two, so I removed it.

Several days passed without a sight of the young cats. Then, just as quietly as they had first come, the gray striped one was there in my front yard. Once again, speaking cat talk, he approached me in a friendly manner. I quickly went and replenished the cereal bow, which I sat in front of the gray. He hunched down over the bowl and nibbled a few bites of the dry cereal, then deciding this wasn't real food, suitable for one of his kind, abandoned the meal and wandered away. I wondered what had happened to the pretty orange cat, which never returned again. But living in the wilds of Madera County, California, small animals are prey for coyotes, bobcats and an occasional cougar.

While doing some shopping at the local market, I thought of getting some real cat food. I bought a box of the kind that TV Commercials say, "brings cats running from all over to imbibe in its kittydeliciousness." I was now ready when my furry little buddy returned. An old plastic tub of chip dip was cleaned up and filled with cat food. I offered it with a flourish and stood back to watch it enjoy real cat food.

Eyeing the food, he eagerly hunkered down before the bowl and began eating. After a couple of bites, he backed off, looked up at me as if to say, "What the hell is this stuff?" Without another bite, he stalked off in a look of indignation.

A few days later, I discovered why he didn't find my kitty food offering acceptable to his palate. Looking out my living room window, there was the young cat on my front walk with a small animal in its mouth. He dropped it on the ground and I could see it was a very alive and kicking gopher. The gopher made a run for it but the cat was in control. Snatching up the gopher once again, with a toss of his head, he threw it into the air and watched as it landed.

Not one to give up easily, mister gopher faced his captor and actually attacked the cat, head on. Kitty jumped back and then began a chase scene worthy of any of Hollywood's finest stunt films. Gopher ran away. Cat chased it. Cat caught gopher. Cat dropped gopher. Gopher ran at cat. Cat ran away. Gopher ran behind a flowerpot. Cat pawed at gopher behind the flowerpot. Gopher ran out from behind the pot. Cat caught gopher and once again tossed gopher into the air and as it landed, decided to have a boxing match with it. Cat threw a left hook. Gopher ducked. Cat threw a right cross. Gopher didn't duck fast enough and took one on the chin.

The novelty evidently wore off and the cat decided it was time to stop playing with its food. With one final bite, he finished the game and began devouring his quarry.

The next morning, looking out onto my back patio, there was the gray cat with yet another gopher, involved in the same game. My offering of commercially prepared cat food may have had the average house cat salivating in anticipation, but to my wilderness bred kitty, if it wasn't live meat, forget it.

So, I used the old plastic chip dip tub to put out fresh water daily, for the gray cat to wash down his gopher meals. I gave thanks that my garden was being protected from subterranean pests.

With winter coming on, I have to figure out a shelter for my hunter so he'll be safe to continue his pursuit of Gopher a la Carte. If he chooses to alter his menu, there is still a whole box of cat food going unused.

AMONG MY SOUVENIRS

When I was a little boy, maybe aged seven or eight, I lived for a time with my father and grandmother. My dad and my mother were divorced and it was agreed that I would live for a while with one of them and then back to the other. I was a gangly, eight year old tennis ball now that I reflect on the times.

I spent a lot of time alone in my grandmother's house as both she and my father worked days. When I was not in school, I had a lot of free time on my hands and spent a lot of it reading. My uncle Gene, Dad's brother, also lived in the house and collected pulp fiction western magazines so my library of cowboy literature was vast.

My Aunt Georgia, had no children of her own and used to lavish her motherly instincts on me, bringing me all kinds of things to keep me occupied. One of her gifts, which I really liked, was a portable record player and several thick 78 rpm records. I remember playing those records over and over. The labels on the records stated the name of the tunes and who the instrumentalists were. Particular favorites of mine were "On The Road To Mandalay" ("Where the flying fishes play, and the dawn comes up like thunder over China 'cross the bay"), and "Among My Souvenirs".

"Among My Souvenirs" was particularly touching to a lonely little boy who, through no fault of his own, was really alone with no permanent, solid family. Especially poignant was the last line where the singer who has recounted all of those mementoes of his life gone by, sings,

"I count them all apart,
And as the tear drops start,
I find a broken heart... among my souvenirs."

The memory of this time of long ago was brought back to mind as I, following a recent divorce from wife number two, was once again with no family. The prior years had some wonderful times with my first family of wife, son and daughter. Then, the dark times, through the sickness and deaths of my mother and father. A divorce marred the picture followed by many years of living alone and accomplishing careers in business and as an actor, choreographer and ultimately a busy stage director. All these events as well as the prior noted ill-fated second marriage.

My home is filled with souvenirs of those times. As I go through my photos, items received as gifts from loving friends and letters and notes from the great and near great, I have cause to remember a time of happiness or heartbreak in connection with each piece.

Photos of old army buddies aboard troop ships heading for the war zone, were bittersweet souvenirs; on an adventure, but away from friends and family once again.

Photos taken in Japan of religious shrines, ox drawn wagons mixed in with modern automobile traffic and a painting of Mt. Fuji on silk reminded me of Mary, a Kansan working with the United States Military Sea Transport Service, who was with me when I took the photos.

In looking through old e-mails I find a series of notes from an old and treasured friend telling of her treatments for a malignant tumor. She asked for prayers and was looking forward, not happily, to chemotherapy accompanied by loss of her hair. She was being fitted for a wig. My e-mail to her telling her that I would be away for a few days but was hoping that all treatments were taking effect and that improvement was happening on a daily basis. Then, upon my return, the e-mail from her husband stating simply, "With great sadness, my Marilyn went home to our Lord on Wednesday, June 30. She went into the hospital on Thursday and passed this Wednesday. Don". So unexpected, so undeserved but oh, so final.

On a happier note, there are photos of second wife Rita and I from a tour to Pompeii with a tame Mount Vesuvius in the background. Another souvenir is a ticket to visit a museum in Rome filled with beautiful artifacts and some photos of a visit to the Vatican. Though a bit cloudy, the Roman sky was otherwise clear as thousands of us inched our way several blocks to the entry of St. Peter's. We stood in line for hours to get inside to view marvelous treasures of paintings and statuary including Michelangelo's sculpture "The Pieta".

We had entered through the right hand doors to St. Peter's, which are known as the Holy Doors, and which are only opened every fifty years. Entrance through these portals is said to ensure the forgiveness of all sins. Thanks, I needed that.

After the tour we left St. Peter's and went across the street to a souvenir shop. Once we were inside, a

CPSIA information can be obtained at www.ICGtesting.com
Printed in the USA
LVOW13s0729070813

346404LV00011B/237/P